THE INDEX OF MIDDLE ENGLISH PROSE

General Editor A. S. G. Edwards
Co-editors N. F. Blake, L. Braswell and R. Hanna III

HANDLIST V
ADDITIONAL COLLECTION (10001-14000),
BRITISH LIBRARY, LONDON

THE INDEX OF MIDDLE ENGLISH PROSE

Advisory Committee

Professor D. Pearsall (*Chairman*)
Professor R.H. Robbins (*Honorary Advisory Editor*)
The late Professor Morton W. Bloomfield
Professor D.S. Brewer
The late Professor E. Talbot Donaldson
Dr A.I. Doyle
Dr Anne Hudson
Professor Alexandra Johnston
Professor Valerie Lagorio
The late Professor R.M. Lumiansky
Mr Malcolm Parkes
The late Professor Elizabeth Salter
Mr R.A. Waldron
Professor Siegfried Wenzel

Already published

Handlist I
The Henry E. Huntington Library
Ralph Hanna III

Handlist II
The John Rylands University Library of Manchester
and Chetham's Library, Manchester
G.A. Lester

Handlist III
The Digby Collection, Bodleian Library, Oxford
Patrick J. Horner

Handlist IV
Douce Manuscripts, Bodleian Library, Oxford
Laurel Braswell

ISSN 0267-2472

THE INDEX OF MIDDLE ENGLISH PROSE

HANDLIST V

*A Handlist of Manuscripts containing Middle English Prose
in the Additional Collection (10001-12000),
British Library, London*

PETER BROWN

*and in the Additional Collection (12001-14000),
British Library, London*

ELTON D. HIGGS

D. S. BREWER

© The Index of Middle English Prose 1988

First published 1988 by D. S. Brewer
240 Hills Road, Cambridge
an imprint of Boydell & Brewer Ltd
PO Box 9, Woodbridge, Suffolk IP12 3DF
and of Boydell & Brewer Inc.
Wolfeboro, New Hampshire 03894-2069, USA

ISBN 0 85991 270 1

British Library Cataloguing in Publication Data

The Index of Middle English prose.
 Handlist 5 : A handlist of manuscripts
 containing Middle English prose in the
 Additional Collection (10001-14000),
 British Library, London
 1. Prose in English, 1066-1400 –
 Bibliographies
 I. Brown, Peter   II. Higgs, Elton D., *1937-*
 III. British Library. *Department of Manuscripts*
 016.828'108
 ISBN 0-85991-270-1

Library of Congress Cataloging-in-Publication Data applied for

Printed and bound in Great Britain by Short Run Press Ltd, Exeter

General Introduction

When work began on the Index of Middle English Prose in 1977, it was agreed that the first step towards the preparation of a comprehensive index would be a series of detailed descriptions of the Middle English prose in various major repositories. Each of these Handlists is designed as a self-contained volume. Each includes a full listing of all Middle English prose items, and full indexing of the majority. A few general features of the Handlist should be noted:

1. Each Handlist provides, in the order of the library's shelfmarks, a listing of all pieces of Middle English prose in the collections. Certain categories of material are noted, but not indexed. These include letters and all legal or quasi-legal documents – deeds, indentures, and other such documents. The existence of such documents is, however, noted as they occur.

2. Macaronic materials appear in an Appendix and are recorded only by opening lines.

3. Each item in the manuscript is identified by an arabic numeral placed within square brackets at the head of the entry. Each manuscript has an independent sequence of numbers. The identifying number is followed by opening and closing lines of the text, located by the folios on which they occur. In citing folios, numerals without further indication denote rectos; ^{a} and ^{b} thus indicate the first and second columns of rectos ($v.^{va}$ and ^{vb} for the same columns on versos). Normally at least fifty words at the beginning of the text appear and at least twenty at the end. Acephalous and atelous texts are treated as normal texts except that they are preceded and/or followed by three dots (...) to indicate incompleteness.

4. Transcriptions represent the "final text version" with marginal and interlinear corrections indicated, although with no notice of cancellations and expunctions. Abbreviations have been silently expanded to accord with the normal full forms of the text. ȝ, when it represents *z*, has been transcribed as *z*. Word-division is editorial, and only the opening word is capitalized (*i.e. ff* has been normalized). Within the transcription, a solidus marks the boundary between two folios or columns.

5. Insofar as these can be differentiated with any confidence from the incipit and explicit of the actual text, opening and/or closing rubrics, shorn of the conventional "Incipit" or "Here begynneth," are recorded within quotation marks. All such manuscript titles are from initial rubrics, except as noted; alternative sources of titles include RT (running title), col (the colophon or explicit), and tab (heading of ms. table of contents). Following this data full bibliographical details are given: underlined, the normal modern title, where one exists; references to standard bibliographical authorities and editions, a description of the work (if unpublished) and the opening lines of important divisions within longer unpublished texts, and references to other manuscripts or to relevant bibliographical sources. Other manuscripts are cited in a fixed order: mss. in London (BL first, other libraries alphabetically), mss. in Oxford (BodL first), mss. in Cambridge (CUL first), mss. in other English libraries (alphabetically by location), mss. in Scotland, mss. in Wales, mss. in Ireland, mss. in the U.S., mss. in Europe, mss. in Asia, mss. in Australia. Texts are located by initial folio only; absence of a folio reference indicates that the work occupies the full ms.

6. Certain categories of material, notably groups of sermons and groups of recipes,

pose particular problems. We have sought to index each sermon separately, but have not attempted this for groups of recipes, giving instead the openings of the initial three recipes and the concluding lines of the final one. Individual recipes in main text-hands are transcribed; those added by later users of the manuscripts are simply noted.

7. Each Handlist closes with an index, the raw material for the eventual Index of Middle English Prose. The index lists, in strictly alphabetical order (*i* and *y*, *u* and *v* are separated; *y* for *þ* appears with / under *th*; ȝ appears after *g*), all incipits, all explicits in reverse order, and all manuscript rubrics. Separate listings provide, as needed, incipits and reverse explicits for acephalous and atelous texts.

8. Our aim is to include all Middle English prose materials composed between c.1200 and c.1500. There are obvious difficulties with establishing either date with any certainty in most instances, particularly as they involve the latter terminus. For the earlier one, we have tended to include anything not described in N. R. Ker's *Catalogue of Manuscripts Containing Anglo-Saxon* (Oxford: Clarendon, 1957). For the latter one, we have sought to err on the side of a generous inclusiveness, feeling that it is better to include some works which might not belong rather than risk omitting them. We also include all post-medieval transcripts of relevant Middle English works.

A. S. G. Edwards
General Editor

Acknowledgements

It was Derek Pearsall who suggested that I might compile one of the Handlists for the *Index of Middle English Prose*. To him thanks are due for an introduction, by this means, to some fascinating areas of Middle English scholarship hitherto dimly known to me. Since then, I have received much help and encouragement from Tony Edwards, Norman Blake and Ralph Hanna, who have saved me from many blunders, inaccuracies and inconsistencies. Like them, Geoffrey Lester and Brian Donaghey read one or more drafts of my work and made many useful suggestions for improvement. Not least among the pleasures of compiling the Handlist has been the contact occasioned with others working on other Handlists or on allied projects. Roger Dahood, Sigmund Eisner, Charlotte Morse, Linda Voigts and Ronald Waldron have all been generous in sharing their extensive knowledge of Middle English texts.

The inter-library loan service at the University of Kent has refused to buckle under the strain of frequent multiple requests and Enid Dixon, who is in charge of the service, has acted upon the most arcane of requirements with great efficiency. The resources of Kent's Special Collection, and the helpful attentions of its librarian, Stephen Holland, have considerably eased the labour of preparing the present volume, while the general cheerfulness of the Kent library staff has created a friendly atmosphere in which to work. To the University of Kent must also go my thanks for helping to defray the cost of numerous train journeys between London and Canterbury.

In making heavy demands on the energies of staff at the British Library I have customarily been met with patience and courtesy, an experience repeated at the University of London Library. Librarians and archivists elsewhere have been prompt in supplying folio references from manuscripts in their care. They include Bruce Barker-Benfield (Bodleian Library, Oxford), Colin A. McLaren (Aberdeen University Library), Jane Maxwell (Trinity College, Dublin), R. I. Page

Acknowledgements

(Corpus Christi College, Cambridge) and R. C. Yorke (College of Arms, London).

The deficiencies of the following Handlist for Additional manuscripts 10001-12000 are entirely my own responsibility, and I shall be grateful to know of any corrections and revisions which are thought necessary.

Peter Brown
English Board
Darwin College
University of Kent
Canterbury
Kent CT2 7NY
England

* * *

I wish to thank Professor Linda Ehrsam Voigts of the University of Missouri-Kansas City and Miss Janet Cowen of King's College, London, for their advice and comments while I was compiling the Handlist for Additional manuscripts 12001-14000. I must also thank Janet Cowen, Ronald Waldron and Peter Brown for each checking several manuscripts for me after I returned to the United States. I should also like to join Peter Brown in acknowledging the courtesy and patience of the staffs of the British Library and the University of London Library.

Elton D. Higgs
Humanities Department
College of Arts, Sciences, and Letters
The University of Michigan-Dearborn
Dearborn, Michigan 48128
U.S.A.

Introduction

The Trustees of the British Library (British Museum as it then was) acquired their first Additional manuscripts in 1756. The sequence of numbers begins at 4101, following on from that of the manuscripts acquired three years earlier from the executors of Sir Hans Sloane.[1] Since 1756 there has been a steady annual accretion of manuscripts in the Additional category, the result of donations, bequests and purchases. At the time of writing (November 1987) the most recent acquisition is numbered 64795.[2]

Originally included in the Additional category were Egyptian, Oriental and Coptic manuscripts, but these were transferred to other departments of the British Museum during the nineteenth century. Additional 10001 to 14000 are thus representative of the series as a whole in being a miscellaneous collection of Western manuscripts from all periods. Prominent among the benefactors in this sector of the collection is the Rt. Rev. Dr Samuel Butler, Lord Bishop of Lichfield (1774-1839), grandfather of the novelist, whose manuscripts were purchased in 1841. The Butler acquisition, Additional 11828 to 12117, contains many medieval works, but includes only two examples of Middle English prose, a Wycliffite New Testament (Add 11858) and a copy of *Brut* (Add 12030).

The first manuscript to appear in these Handlists, Additional 10036, was acquired in 1836, and the last, Additional 12195, in 1841. Thus the majority of books here represented came to the British Museum through the hands of Sir Frederic Madden (1801-73), Keeper of Manuscripts from 1837 to 1866, a dynamic period in the history of the institution which he served. (He had been an Assistant Keeper since 1828.) Madden, one of the great nineteenth-century palaeographers, pursued an energetic policy of acquisition and supervised the cataloguing of the material in his care. Students of Middle English writings have good reason to be thankful to him.[3]

There is no published descriptive catalogue for

Introduction

Additional manuscripts 10001 to 10012, but they are included in an index and in an Annual List of manuscripts acquired.[4] From Additional 10013 to 14000 there are published working catalogues, based on the Annual Lists.[5] The catalogues contain short descriptions (often in Latin) and have remained unrevised since they first appeared some one hundred and fifty years ago. They can therefore be used only as preliminary guides to content and so are not cited in the Handlist annotations.

Approximately one third of Additional manuscripts 10001-12000 are medieval. Of these a considerable number were not examined. The manuscripts passed over contain works, such as Italian humanist and Icelandic compositions, thought least likely to contain examples of Middle English prose. However, the shortcomings of the catalogue entailed a relatively high level of spot-checking. In all, 411 manuscripts were scanned, and of these twenty yielded a total of eighty-one Middle English prose items. In Additional manuscripts 12001-14000 there is a much lower proportion of medieval works, and almost all of the appropriate manuscripts were examined (a total of 100 volumes). Only four contain significant passages of Middle English prose, giving a further nineteen items. All of those manuscripts which were scanned without success are listed at the end of the present volume.

As might be expected from a large and miscellaneous collection of this kind, the items found exemplify virtually every type of Middle English prose composition. Religious works form the largest category. Here the most substantial pieces are Nicholas Love's translation from pseudo-Bonaventura, *Myrrour of the Blessed Lyf of Jesu Christ*, and the here unattributed translation of Voragine's legends of the saints, the *Gilte Legende* (both in Add 11565). Other attributed devotional works include the Prologue of Richard Rolle's English Psalter (Add 10046), a translation of his *Oleum Effusum* with Walter Hilton's *Scale of Perfection*

Introduction

(Add 11748), and Hilton's *Eight Chapters on Perfection* with Edmund of Abingdon's *Mirror of Saint Edmund* (Add 10053). Wycliffite translations of the Bible occur (Add 10046, 10047, 10596 and 11858), as do treatises for parish priests (Add 10036 and 10053). Other anonymous pious compositions include the eschatalogical *Vision of St Paul* (a unique copy) with *Of Three Arrows on Doomsday* (Add 10036) and the *Book of the Craft of Dying* (Add 10596), numerous prayers (Add 10596), and such miscellaneous items as a treatise on the Seven Deadly Sins, the Letter of St Jerome to Demetriades and a fragment of *Dives and Pauper* (Add 10053) and Letter of Lentulus on the physiognomy of Christ (Add 10106).

The chief representatives of secular works are Chaucer's *Boece* (Add 10340) and the *Brut* (Add 10099 and Add 12030). Other works with an historical bent include a genealogy of Edward IV (Add 10099), and a petition to the King and *Manner and Form of the Coronation*, both in Additional 10106. The major scientific compositions are William of Saliceto's On Anatomy, the Little Treatise on Surgery by Lanfranc of Milan and the anonymous Judgement of Urine, all in one manuscript (Add 10440); Lanfranc's *Science of Cirurgie* and a herbal derived from Macer (Add 12056); and a "health book" by Johannes Paulinus, *The Booke of Astronomye and of Philosophye*, a handbook of gynaecology and the Book of Ypocras (Add 12195). The last three manuscripts also contain medical recipes and charms. There are further medical recipes in Add 10336, in which macaronic musical material features as part of *De Arte Musica* by John Tucke. Another technical composition, in a fragmentary state, is *Accedence*, a grammar based on Donatus (Add 12195).

The existence of most of the above items is well known, and many of the texts have been published or collated. However, one or two have been overlooked and a number remain unedited. Thus the Sentence of Cursing in Additional 11579 is a copy not hitherto noticed, and the same appears to be true of The Rule of the Life of Our Lady (Add 11748), excerpted from Love's *Myrrour*, and of an excerpt from the General Prologue to the Wycliffite Bible (Add 10046). Two interesting texts in Additional 10106, A Good Tretys to Gode Levyng, and Temptations of the Devil, have not received the attentions of an editor, an omission which I hope to remedy in the near future. Nor does there appear to be an edition of On Anatomy by William of Saliceto (Add 10440). The prayers of Additional 10596 likewise merit publication.

The procedures used in compiling the following Handlists are in line with those previously established, with two exceptions. For ease of use, the Index of Reverse Explicits is no longer combined with the Index of Incipits and Rubrics, but appears separately. This procedural change will be standard in subsequent Handlists. A further innovation is the Summary List of Contents, providing at a glance the titles of texts contained within individual manuscripts.

Peter Brown

Notes

[1] T. C. Skeat, *The Catalogues of the Manuscript Collections in the British Museum*, rev. edn., (London: Trustees of the British Museum, 1962), pp. 2-8; and M. A. E. Nickson, *The British Library: Guide to the Catalogues and Indexes of the Department of Manuscripts*, 2nd. edn. (London: British Library Board, 1982), p. 7.
[2] "'Rough Register' of Acquisitions of the Department of Manuscripts British Library 1986-," in progress (typescript in looseleaf available in the Department of Manuscripts).
[3] Robert W. Ackerman and Gretchen P. Ackerman, *Sir Frederic Madden: A Biographical Sketch and Bibliography*, Garland Reference Library of the Humanities, Vol. 126, (New York and London: Garland, 1979). For a general history of the

Introduction

library during Madden's service, see Edward Miller, *Prince of Librarians: The Life and Times of Antonio Panizzi of the British Museum*, (London: André Deutsch, 1967); and his *That Noble Cabinet: A History of the British Museum*, (London: André Deutsch, 1973), chs. 5-7. The earlier history is by Arundell Esdaile, *The British Museum Library: A Short History and Survey*, (London: George Allen & Unwin, 1946).

[4] *Index to the Additional Manuscripts ... acquired in the years 1783-1835*, (London: Printed by Order of the Trustees, 1849); and *Catalogue of Additional Manuscripts. Nos. 6666-10018* (made up from printed Annual Lists of manuscripts acquired 1828-1835).

[5] *List of Additions to the Manuscripts in the British Museum in the Years 1836-1840*, (London: Printed by Order of the Trustees, 1843); and *Catalogue of Additions to the Manuscripts in the British Museum in the Years 1841-1845*, (London: Printed by Order of the Trustees, 1850).

Abbreviations

Add	Additional MS
AEB	*Analytical and Enumerative Bibliography*
Allen, *Writings Ascr*	Emily Hope Allen. *Writings Ascribed to Richard Rolle Hermit of Hampole and Materials for His Biography*. Modern Languages Association of America, Monograph ser., 3. New York: Heath; London: Oxford Univ. Press, 1927.
BJRL	*Bulletin of the John Rylands Library*
BL	British Library, London
BodL	Bodleian Library, Oxford
Braswell	Laurel Braswell. *The Index of Middle English Prose. Handlist IV: Douce Manuscripts ... in the Bodleian Library, Oxford*. Cambridge: Brewer 1988.
Camb	Cambridge (to introduce a sequence of Cambridge libraries)
CCC	Corpus Christi College
Col	College
CUL	Cambridge University Library
Doyle, "Work"	A. I. Doyle. "The Work of a Late Fifteenth-Century Scribe, William Ebesham." *BJRL*, 39 (1956-57), 298-325.
EETS es	Early English Text Society, extra series
EETS os	Early English Text Society, original series
Eng	English (MS)
ESt	*Englische Studien*
F-M	Josiah Forshall and Frederick Madden, eds. *The Holy Bible, containing the Old and New Testaments, with the Apocryphal Books, in the Earliest English Versions Made from the Latin Vulgate by John Wycliffe and His Followers*. 4 vols. Oxford: Oxford Univ. Press, 1850.
Hamer	Richard Hamer, ed. *Three Lives from the Gilte Legende*. Edited from MS BL Egerton 876. Middle English Texts, vol. 9. Heidelberg: Winter, 1978.
Hanna	Ralph Hanna III. *The Index of Middle English Prose. Handlist I: The Henry E. Huntington Library*. Cambridge: Brewer, 1984.
Heinrich	Fritz Heinrich. *Ein mittelenglisches Medizinbuch*. Halle: Niemeyer, 1896.

Abbreviations

Hudson, "Contributions"	Anne Hudson. "Contributions to a Bibliography of Wycliffite Writings." *NQ*, 218 (1973), 443-53.
Hudson, *Selections*	----------, ed. *Selections from English Wycliffite Writings*. Cambridge: Cambridge Univ. Press, 1978.
IMEV	Carleton Brown and Rossell Hope Robbins. *The Index of Middle English Verse*. New York: Columbia Univ. Press for the Index Society, 1943.
IPMEP	R. E. Lewis, N. F. Blake and A. S. G. Edwards. *Index of Printed Middle English Prose*. Garland Reference Library of the Humanities, Vol. 537. New York and London: Garland, 1985.
Jolliffe	P. S. Jolliffe. *A Check-List of Middle English Prose Writings of Spiritual Guidance*. Subsidia Mediaevalia, 2. Toronto: Pontifical Institute of Mediaeval Studies, 1974.
JRL	John Rylands Library, Manchester
Ker, *Medieval Libraries*	N. R. Ker. *Medieval Libraries of Great Britain: A List of Surviving Books*. 2nd edn. Royal Historical Society Guides and Handbooks, No. 3. London Royal Historical Society, 1964.
Lamb Pal Libr	Lambeth Palace Library
Lester	G. A. Lester. *The Index of Middle English Prose. Handlist II: Manuscripts containing Middle English Prose in the John Rylands Library of Manchester and Chetham's Library, Manchester*. Cambridge: Brewer, 1985.
Libr	Library
Lindberg	Conrad Lindberg. "The Manuscripts and Versions of the Wycliffite Bible: A Preliminary Survey." *SN*, 42 (1970), 333-47.
LSE	*Leeds Studies in English*
Magd	Magdalen(e)
Maskell	William Maskell. *Monumenta Ritualia Ecclesiae Anglicanae, or Occasional Offices of the Church of England According to the Ancient Use of Salisbury, the Prymer in English and Other Prayers and Forms, with Dissertations and Notes*. 3 vols. London: Pickering, 1846-47.
Matheson	Lister M. Matheson. "The Middle English Prose *Brut*: A Location List of the Manuscripts and Early Printed

Abbreviations

	Editions." *AEB*, 3 (1979), 254-66.
MEP	A. S. G. Edwards, ed. *Middle English Prose: A Critical Guide to Major Authors and Genres*. New Brunswick, N.J.: Rutgers Univ. Press, 1984.
Misc	Miscellaneous MS.
M-R	John M. Manly and Edith Rickert, eds. *The Text of the Canterbury Tales Studied on the Basis of All Known Manuscripts*. 8 vols. Chicago and London: Univ. of Chicago Press, 1940.
NM	*Neuphilologische Mitteilungen*
NQ	*Notes & Queries*
Oxon	Oxford (to introduce a sequence of Oxford libraries)
Powell	Lawrence F. Powell, ed. *The Mirrour of the Blessed Lyf of Jesu Christ ...* (Oxford: Clarendon Press, 1908)
Rawl	Rawlinson MS
Revell	Peter Revell, comp. *Fifteenth Century English Prayers and Meditations: A Descriptive List of Manuscripts in the British Library*. Garland Reference Library of the Humanities, No. 19. New York and London: Garland, 1975.
Robbins	Rossell Hope Robbins. "Medical Manuscripts in Middle English." *Speculum*, 45 (1970), 393-415.
SN	*Studia Neophilologica*
STC	A. W. Pollard, G. R. Redgrave, et al., comps. *A Short-Title Catalogue of Books Printed in England, Scotland, and Ireland and of English Books Printed Abroad 1475-1640*. 2nd edn., comps. W. A. Jackson, F. S. Ferguson, and Katherine F. Pantzer. 2 vols. London: Bibliographical Society, 1976-86.
TCol	Trinity College
Thomson	David Thomson. *An Edition of the Middle English Grammatical Texts*. New York and London: Garland, 1984.
Thomson, *Descriptive Catalogue*	——————. *A Descriptive Catalogue of Middle English Grammatical Texts*. New York and London: Garland, 1979.
UCol	University College
UL	University Library
Well Hist Med Libr	Wellcome History of Medicine Library, London
Wells Rev	J. Burke Severs and Albert E. Hartung, eds. *A Manual of the Writings in Middle English 1050-1500*.

Abbreviations

7 vols., in progress. New Haven: Connecticut Academy of Arts and Sciences, 1967-.

Summary List of Contents

Add 10036 [1] *The Vision of St Paul*
          [2] *Of Three Arrows on Doomsday*
          [3] *Sacerdos Parochialis*

Add 10046 [1] Richard Rolle, Prologue to his English Psalter
          [2] General Prologue to the Wycliffite Bible
          [3] Wycliffite Book of Psalms
          [4] Twelve Canticles

Add 10047 [1] Wycliffite Psalms 1-73

Add 10052 [A1] Fifth Tabula of the *Speculum Christiani*
          [A2] Sixth Tabula of the *Speculum Christaini*

Add 10053 [1] *The Mirror of St Edmund*
          [2] The Seven Works of Spiritual Mercy
          [3] The Five Inner Wits
          [4] Walter Hilton, *Eight Chapters on Perfection*
          [5] Letter of St Jerome to Demetriades
          [6] The Seven Deadly Sins
          [7] *Dives and Pauper*
          [8] *Sacerdos Parochialis*

Add 10099 [1] *Brut*
          [2] Genealogy of Edward IV
          [3] Chronicle Notes

Add 10106 [1] Petition to the King
          [2] *Manner and Form of the Coronation*
          [3] *Privilege of Westmynstre*
          [4] Table of the Feyth of Christian People
          [5] A Good Tretys to Gode Levyng
          [6] Temptations of the Devil
          [7] Letter of Lentulus
          [8] Marginal words

Add 10336 [1] Medical recipe
          [A3] John Tucke, *De Arte Musica*
          [2] Medical recipes

Add 10340 [1] Geoffrey Chaucer, *Boece*

Add 10440 [1] William of Saliceto, On Anatomy
          [2] Medical recipes
          [3] Lanfranc of Milan, Little Treatise on Surgery
          [4] Medical recipes
          [5] The Judgement of Urine
          [6] Medical recipes

Add 10596 [1] *The Book of the Craft of Dying*
          [2] Wycliffite *Tobit*
          [3] Wycliffite Magnificat
          [4] Wycliffite Benedictus

Contents

            [5] Devout Meditation on the Goodness of God
            [6] Prayer to God
            [7] Prayer to Christ
            [8] Prayer to St Michael the Archangel
            [9] Prayer to Michael the Archangel
          [10] Prayer to Gabriel the Archangel
          [11] Prayer to Raphael the Archangel
          [12] Prayer to a Guardian Angel
          [13] Prayer to a Guardian Angel
          [14] Prayer to a Guardian Angel
          [15] Prayer to a Guardian Angel
          [16] Prayer to All Angels
          [17] Prayer to All Angels
          [18] Prayer to Apostles and Evangelists
          [19] Prayer to Apostles and Evangelists
          [20] Prayer to Holy Patriarchs
          [21] Prayer to the Holy Innocents
          [22] Prayer to Martyrs
          [23] Prayer to Confessors
          [24] Prayer to Virgins
          [25] Prayer to Maidens
          [26] Prayer to All Saints
          [27] Prayer to All Saints
          [28] Prayer to All Saints
          [29] *The Pistle of Holy Susannah*

Add 10628 *[1] Miscellaneous endpaper notes and inventory

Add 11301 [1] Letter to the Archbishop of Canterbury
          [2] Letter to King Henry VI

Add 11304 [1] Miscellaneous annotations

Add 11305 *[1] Miscellaneous annotations

Add 11307 *[1] Miscellaneous words

Add 11565 [1] Nicholas Love, *Myrrour of the Blessed Lyf of Jesu Christ*
          [2] *1438 Golden Legend (Gilte Legende)*

Add 11579 [1] Sentence of Cursing

Add 11748 [1] Walter Hilton, *The Scale of Perfection*
          [2] Translation of Richard Rolle, *Oleum Effusum*
          [3] Nicholas Love, The Rule of the Life of Our Lady

Add 11858 [1] Wycliffite New Testament

Add 12030 [1] *Brut*

Add 12056 [1] The Virtues of Herbs
          [2] Lanfranc of Milan, *Science of Cirurgie*

xix

Contents

             [3] Medical recipes
             [4] Medical recipes

Add 12193 [1] Note signed by Henry VI

Add 12195 [1] *Accedence*
             [2] Charm
             [3] Charm
             [4] Translation of Johannes Paulinus, *Experimenta de corio serpentis*
             [5] Charms and scientific recipes
             [6] *The Booke of Astronomye and of Philosophye*
             [7] Medical recipes
             [8] Charm and medical recipes
             [9] Astrological treatise
            [10] Medical recipes
            [11] The Charm of St William, other charms, and medical recipes
            [12] Handbook of Gynaecology
            [13] Book of Ypocras

London
The British Library
Additional Manuscripts

Add 10036
Described: George H. McKnight, ed., *King Horn, Floriz and Blauncheflur, The Assumption of Our Lady*, EETS, os 14 (1866), p. lv; J. A. Herbert, ed., *Titus and Vespasian, or The Destruction of Jerusalem*, (London: Roxburghe Club, 1905), pp. xxvii-xxx; H. L. D. Ward and J. A. Herbert, *Catalogue of Romances in the Department of Manuscripts in the British Museum*, 3 vols., (London: British Museum, 1883-1910), I: 187-89; Gisela Guddat-Figge, *Catalogue of Manuscripts containing Middle English Romances*, Münchener Universitäts-Schriften, band 4, (München: Fink, 1976), pp. 143-44.

[1]
f. 81
Poule and myȝel praied to oure lord ihesu crist of his gret grace to schewe þe peynes to his disciple poule þat he myȝt declare hem in openyng to cristen peple wherefore oure lord graunted him power bi þe leding of his aungel michael for to se þe peynes of soules ypynsched in þat ferful place ...
f. 85
... and þer to euery man hadde foure tounges of iren ne myȝt nouȝt telle how fele sorwes þer ben in helle and so sodeynliche þei wente fro þat place

"A questioun of þe peynes of helle and how soules desireþ to haue rest in þat place," f. 81, [*The Vision of Saint Paul*]; s. xiv/xv; Revell, 186.
Edition and Other MSS: Wells Rev, 7: 646 [320]; *IPMEP*, 535; edited from this MS by E. Kölbing, "Eine bisher unbekante ME. Version von Pauli Höllenfahrt," *ESt*, 22 (1896), 134-39.

[2]

Add 10036

f. 85

Who so wol haue in mynde þe dredeful daie of dome so þat we
mowe be moued with drede to fle fro synne as þe wise man
biddeþ his sone seiynge þus memorare novissima [margin
Ecclesiasticus 7⁰] et in eternum non peccabis þat is haue
mynde on þe laste þinges þat is þe daie of dome and hit
schal kepe þee fro synne ...

f. 91

... ffor as ofte as ȝe diden þise þinges to þe lest of myn
ȝe diden to me to þat blessed hond and kyngdom and ioie
euerlastynge bringe vs ihesu cryst þat bouȝtist man with þi
precyous bloode mercyful god amen

"þe þre arowis þat god schal schete at domysdaie apon hem
þat schullen be dampned," f. 85, [*Of Three Arrows on
Doomsday*]; s. xv in.

Editions and Other MSS: *IPMEP*, 842.

[3]

f. 91ᵛ

In þe pater noster ben seuen askynges þat god him self
ordeyned nedeful for lyf and soule þat eueryche crysten man
is biholde to knowe and for to praie to god in þis wise
prima peticio pater noster qui es in celis sanctificetur
nomen tuum ...

f. 96

... fede þe hungri ȝyue him drinke þat is aþurst visite
him þat is sike herborwe him þat haþ nede cloþe him þat is
naked comfort him þat is in prisoun burie þe cristen þat ben
dede

[*Sacerdos Parochialis*]; instructional tract of basic
commonplaces providing in sequence an exposition of the
Pater Noster (as above); "Salutacio beate marie Ave maria et
cetera haile be þou marie ful of grace" (with a note on
indulgences), f. 92; fragment of a tract on the seven deadly

sins (lacking the section on Pride), "... sleynge hurtyng
fiȝtynge chiding pledynge fals domes," f. 93; "Decem
precepta ueteris testamenti honora domini deum The furst of
godes ten hestes is þat þou schalt honour o god," f. 94; and
"Septem opera misericordie The seuene werkes of mercy ben of
godes heste in þe gospel of seynt mathew," f. 96; s. xv in;
Revell, 281 (part only, f. 92ʳ⁻ᵛ); unedited.
Other MSS: Wells Rev, 7: 2494 [22].

Add 10046
Described: F-M, I: xliv.

[1]
f. 2ᵃ
Greet abundaunce of gostly counfort and ioie in god comiþ in
þe hertis of hem þat seien or syngen deuoutli þese salmes in
preisyng of ihesu crist þei droppen swetnesse in mannes
soule and holden delite in here þouȝtis and tenden here
willis wiþ þe fier of loue makynge hem hoote in charite ...
4ᵛᵃ
... and ofte rehersiþ þe stories of þe elde testament and
bryngiþ in þe kepyng of goddis heestis and loue of enemyes

"a prologe on þe salmes of þe sauter," f. 2ᵃ, [Richard
Rolle, Prologue to his English Psalter]; ends: "ende
prologe," f. 4ᵛᵃ; s. xv.
Editions and Other MSS: Wells Rev, 2: 538 [12]; *IPMEP*, 271;
items [1]-[5] also appear in the same sequence in HM 501
(Hanna, pp. 27-28).

[2]
f. 4ᵛᵃ
But it is to wite þat holy scripture haþ iiij
vndirstondyngis leteral allegorik moral and anagogik þe
leteral vndirstondyng techyþ þe þing doon in deede and

Add 10046

literal vndirstonding is ground and foundment of þre goostli
vndirstondyngis in so moche as austyn to vincent and oþir
doctouris seyn oonly bi þe literal vndirstonding a man may
argue aȝens an aduersarie ...
f. 4ᵛᵇ
   ... what vicis þei owen to fle anagogik is a goostly
vndirstonding þat techiþ men what blisse þei schal haue in
heuene

[General Prologue to the Wycliffite Bible (excerpt from ch.
12)]; s. xv²/⁴.
<u>Editions and Other MSS</u> (of General Prologue and of
selections from it): BL Harley 1666, f. 111 (F-M, I: 43);
Oxon, BodL Bodley 277, f. 1; UCol 96, f. 88; Camb, CUL Kk.
1. 8, f. 27; Mm. 2. 15, f. 289 (ch. 15 in Hudson,
Selections, pp. 67-72); CCC 147, f. 17; Dublin, TCol 75, f.
249; San Marino, HM 501, f. 24 (Hanna, p. 27); [*STC* 25587.5
and 25588].

[3]
f. 5ᵃ
Beatus vir qui non abiit in consilio impiorum et in via
peccatorum non stetit et in cathedra pestilencie non sedit
blessid is þe man þat ȝede not in the counceil of wickede
men and stood not in þe weye of synneris and saat not in þe
chaier of pestilence but his wille is in þe lawe of þe lord
   ...
f. 115ᵛᵇ
   ... herie ȝe him in symbalis sownynge wel herie ȝe him in
cymbalis of iubilatioun ech spirit herie þe lord

"þe sauter," f. 115ᵛᵇ, [The Book of Psalms (Wycliffite
later version)]; title and opening verse of each Psalm in
Latin; one quire (ff. 13-20ᵛ) misbound; s. xv²/⁴.
<u>Editions and Other MSS</u>: Wells Rev, 2: 547 [52]; *IPMEP*, 119;
Lester, pp. 27-28.

[4]

f. 115ᵛᵇ

Confitebor tibi domine [margin isaias 12] quoniam iratus es michi conuersus est furor tuus et consolatus es me lord i schal knowleche to þe for þou were wrooþ to me þi strong veniaunce is turned and þou hast confortid me lo god is my sauiour i schal do feiþfully and i schal not drede ...

f. 132ᵇ

... þe hiȝer prelatis as popis cardinalis and bischopis schulde more speciali konne þis crede and teche it to men undir hem explicit

"þe canticlis," f. 115ᵛᵇ, [Twelve Canticles]; opening verse of each Canticle in Latin (incipits included in index); s. xv²ᐟ⁴.

Editions and Other MSS: For first six Canticles in Wycliffite later version see Wells Rev, 2: 547 [52]; *IPMEP*, 119; and F-M, I: xliv; for versions of others from the Prymer see Maskell, II: 18-20 and 233-34 (Benedicite), 229-32 (Te deum), 25-26 and 237 (Benedictus), and 236 (Nunc dimittis); for Athanasian Creed from Rolle's English Psalter and commentary see Wells Rev. 2: 538 [12]; edited excerpts from this MS by G. D. W. Ommaney, *A Critical Dissertation on the Athanasian Creed: Its Original Language, Date, Authorship, Title, Text, Reception, and Use*, (Oxford: Clarendon Press, 1897), pp. 263-65, 308-9, and 544-46.

Add 10047

Described: F-M, I: xliv.

[1]

f. 1

Beatus vir qui non abiit in consilio impiorum et in uia peccatorum non stetit et in cathedra pestelence non sedit

Add 10053

blessid is the man þat ȝede not in þe counceil of wickid men and stood not in þe wey of synneris ne sat not in the chaire of pestelence but his wille is in þe lawe of þe lord ...
f. 149ᵛ
... be thou myndeful of thy schenschipis eiþer vpbreydyngis of tho that ben al day of the vnwise man forȝete thow not the vois of þine enemyes the pride of hem that haten þee stieþ euere

"the psaumes of dauith þat is clepid þe sauter," f. 1, [Psalms 1-73 (Wycliffite later version)]; first verse of each Psalm in Latin; s. xv/xvi.
<u>Editions and Other MSS</u>: Wells Rev, 2: 547 [52]; *IPMEP*, 119; Hudson, "Contributions," p. 450, for related MSS.

Add 10053

[1]
f. 4
Se ȝe ȝoure clepyng þis worde of þe apostil longiþ to ȝow men and wymen of cristes relygyon se ȝe he sayth wherto ȝe ben clepyd and þat he sayth for to stere yow to perfeccion and þerfore whan i thynke on my selfe by day or by nyȝt in that oon half i haue grete joy ...
f. 29
... ffor our loue be loued and for our lownes be hyȝed to þe joȝe of heuen þat is ordeyned for vs

"Speculum sancti edmundi archiopiscopi here begyinnyt þe sermon of saynt edmund of pounteney þat ys clepyd þe merour of saynt edmunde and men clepen it þe merour of holy chyrche," f. 3, [*The Mirror of St Edmund*]; table of contents, f. 3; ends: "amen for his grete pyte and grace," f. 29; s. xv med.
<u>Editions and Other MSS</u>: *IPMEP*, 800.

Add 10053

[2]

f. 29

Teche þe vnkunnynge men goddys lawe counsyle þe vnwyse þe
wey to heuen chastyse rebellyours aȝens goddys hestes
counfort hem þat been in myschefe fforȝeue þyne enemie
worngys [sic] suffer men þat been malencolyouse pray for
þyn enemyis

"Tese [sic] been þe vij werkes of mercy gostly," f. 29, [The
Seven Works of Spiritual Mercy (complete)]; ends: "quod j
pery," f. 29; s. xv med.
Other versions: BL Add 60577, f. 187; Manchester, JRL Eng
85, f. 19; Edinburgh, UL 93, f. 80; New York, Pierpont
Morgan 861, f. 5. Cf. Wells Rev, 7: 2517 [50].

[3]

f. 29

Mynde vnderstondyng wylle reson and ymagynacioun haue mynde
of þe blesse of heuen and eke on þe paynes of helle
vnderstonde what benefetis god haþ don for þe and hou
vnkende þou art aȝen wylle þou þat þe wylle off gode be
fulfyllyd before þyn oune wyll resonably rule þy selfe
vnder þe forme of goodys lawe and alle þo þat been vndir þe
ymagyne goodenesse of oþer men more þan of þyself

"þese been þe v gostly wyttys," f. 29, [The Five Inner
Wits (complete)]; s. xv. med.
Other versions: Wells Rev, 7: 2536 [156], to which may be
added BL Add 60577, f. 131; Lamb Pal Libr 408, f. 5; Oxon,
BodL Laud Misc 23, f.42; Manchester, JRL Eng 85, f. 13ᵛ; New
York, Pierpont Morgan 861, f. 5ᵛ.

[4]

f. 29ᵛ

The ferst token of loue is þat tho louer submitte fully hys
wylle to the wylle of hym that louith and thys special loue

hath thre werkinges the first is if that he þat is loued be
symple and pore meke and in despite þan he þat loueth
couetith to be foule pore and meke ...
f. 40

... goten by the whoundes of crist in the maner before
seide saue vs and kepe vs and cristen men and whomen amen
purcharyte

"a tretes necessarye for men þat ȝeven hem vnto
perfeccioun whiche was foundyn in maister lowys de
fontibus bok at cambrigge and torned in to englisshe be
maister water hilton chanon of thorgortoun," f. 29, [Walter
Hilton, *Eight Chapters on Perfection*,]; s. xv med.
<u>Editions and Other MSS</u>: *IPMEP*, 677; provenance: Augustinian
priory of Holy Trinity, Aldgate (Ker, *Medieval Libraries*, p.
123).

[5]
f. 40ᵛ
The first besynesse and the first studie of a mayden ought
for to be to knowe the wille of our lord and for to enqueren
besili what pleseth hym or what dispLeysed hym so that after
the bidding of the appostel she might yelden hir seruice to
jhesu quemful and resonable ...
f. 68ᵛ

... in thys take thi slepe on the night and atte first
waking þat it falle sone in þi mynde trauaile is short but
the rest is endeles to that reste bringe vs he that for vs
deide vpon the rode tree amen purcharite

"a pystyl of seynt ierome sent to a mayden dematriad þat
hadde vowyd schastite to oure lord ihesu crist," f. 40ᵛ,
[Letter of St Jerome to Demetriades]; some folios out of
sequence; s. xv med.
<u>Other MSS</u>: Jolliffe, H. 5.

Add 10053

[6]

f. 85

Euery cristen man and woman that ȝernyth to be saued hath grete nede to be ware and eschewe the fendis slyȝtthys and nameli to knowe the vij principal sinnys with alle here comune branches the wyche in thys lytyl tretis shortly ben entitlid to warne hym that is vnlerned how lyghtly and in how many diuerse maneris his concience may be cauȝt ...

f. 94ᵛ

... a dedeli sinne ffro the wych he vs kepe that with his precius hert blode owre sowlis dere abowte

[The Seven Deadly Sins]; s. xv med; unedited.
<u>Other MSS</u>: Jolliffe, F. 4.

[7]

f. 94ᵛ

Ferst take hede what veniaunce god hath taken for symple fornycacioun we fyndyn in holy writ genesis xxxiiij that dyna the douȝtir of jacob wente ffrom home to sen þe wommen of that cuntre and to sen here tyre than sichem þe son of emor prince of the cuntre went and defyled þis dyna be nyȝth ...

f. 98ᵛ

... þe sauante knowynge þe wyl of hys lorde and not doynge hys wyl shal ben harde punsched also for his vnkyndenesse for whi þe grete his benefice is and þe more ...

[*Dives and Pauper* (chs. 16-18 of Commandment 6 with ch. 18 incomplete)]; cf. Priscilla Heath Barnum, ed., *Dives and Pauper*, EETS, os 280 (1980), pp. 104-10; s. xv med.
<u>Edition and Other MSS</u>: Wells Rev, 7: 2515 [45]; *IPMEP*, 156.

[8]

f. 99

Add 10099

ʒe shul bileue that þe pater noster þat crist him silf tauʒt to alle cristen men passith alle oþer prayers in these thre poyntis in auctorite in sotelte and profite of alle holi chirch hit passith in auctorite for crist bothe god and man made hit for cristen men to vse hit ...
f. 114
   ... in this maner wise þou shalt loue god holdyng hestis for loue of hym and not for drede of payne

"Sacerdos parochialis tenetur per canones docere et predicare in lingua materna in anno," f. 99, [*Sacerdos Parochialis*]; after the first item, an exposition of the "Pater noster," follow (with rubrics) "Sequitur salutatio angelica Ave maria et cetera heyl be þou marie ful of grace," f. 102; "Sequitur symbalum fidei Credo in deum patrem omnipotentem i beleue in god fadir almighti," f. 103; "De decem preceptis veteris testamenti Honora dominum deum tuum the first of goddys ten heestys," f. 105; "De septem peccatis mortalibus Seuen dedly synnes beþ þese pride enuie wrath slawht couetise glotenye and lecherie," f. 106ᵛ; "De septem operibus misericordis Seuen werkys of mercy euery cristen creatur shal be exampned of," f. 107ᵛ; "De septem virtutibus principalibus Seuen principal vertuis longging to mannis soule bith these," f. 107ᵛ; "De semptem [*sic*] sacramentis ecclesie Seuen sacramentis of holy chirche byth these þe furst sacrament is cristendom," f. 108ᵛ; "De duobus preceptis euangelicis Crist in the gospel fulfilleth al þe lawe into hestis and seith thus," f. 113; s. xv med; unedited except for Pater Noster.
Edition and Other MSS: Wells Rev, 7: 2508 [33] for edition and other MSS of Pater Noster, and 7: 2494 [22] for other MSS of complete treatise; and see BL Royal 8. F. vii, f. 41ᵛ; and Oxon, UCol 28, f. 48.

Add 10099

[1]

f. 11

In the noble land of surey þer was a noble kyng and a man of gret renown that men callid dioclician that wel and worthely gouerened him and keped him thorow his noble chivalry so þat he conquered al þe landes about him so þat almoste al þe kynges of þe world to him wer entendant ...

f. 203

... which in thise dayes is fore mynnshed by þe puissance of þe thurkes and hethen men and þat after þis present and short life we may come to þe euerlastyng life amen explicit

[*Brut* (continued to the coronation of Edward IV)]; table of contents, f. 1; s. xv$^{3/4}$.

Edition and Other MSS: *IPMEP*, 374; and see Matheson, emended and extended in his "Historical Prose," in *MEP*, pp. 232-33; and in his "Printer and Scribe: Caxton, the *Polychronicon*, and the *Brut*," *Speculum*, 60 (1985), p. 593, n. 3. Ff. 181-203 edited from this MS by Friedrich W. D. Brie, *The Brut, or: The Chronicles of England*, EETS, os 136 (1908), pp. 491-33.

[2]

f. 205

In primis it is for to be considred that in þe yere of our lorde godd viijc^{lxxvj} and at that tyme allured being kynge of englonde a famous knight born in danmark calledd rouland and he at þat tyme beinge a panyme vncristened with his hooste entred into ffraunce and conquered roone ...

f. 210^v

... and put þe said edwarde the thrid frome his rightful and lawfulle enheritaunce of þe crown of ffraunce nat considerynge nor remembringe the punysshment that oure lorde god hath ordeyned for thame þat occupie and justefie such maner open wronges

Add 10106

"This breue tretise is compiled for to bringe the people oute of doute that han nat herd of the cronycles and of the lineal descensse vnto the crownes of englande of ffraunce of castel legions and vnto þe duchis of normandie sith it was first conquest and made," f. 205, [Genealogy of Edward IV (concerning his claim to the French throne)]; before 1475, on internal evidence; unedited.
Also in: BL Harley 2252, f. 51ᵛ.

[3]
f. 210ᵛ
Title of þe crown of ffraunce is put vpon some lordes to be determyned within þe yeer also dolfyn of ffraunce shal wed oon of oure kingis doughtres hir iunctis shal be lxij^{librum} the charge of þe mariage at þe costes of þe kinge of ffraunce also our souereyn lorde þe kinge ...
f. 210ᵛ
... oure souereyn lord þe king wil come to englond þer is perviaunce made for his commyng at calais ayenst our lady day

[Chronicle Notes (on Edward IV's title to the French throne and on the betrothal of the King's daughter (Elizabeth) to the French dauphin (Charles) after Edward's expedition to France)]; ca. 1475, on internal evidence; unedited.

Add 10106

[1]
f. 2
"To the kyng oure souerain lord," [Petition to the King (for confirmation of privileges of the Abbot and Convent of Westminster)]; s. xv/xvi.

[2]

Add 10106

f. 21
First the prince that is newe to be crowned the day before
his coronacioun shalle be appareild and clothed with moost
noble and fairest clothing and so he shalle ride from the
toure of london vnto his palace at westmynster thorughoute
þe cite of london barehede ridying with hym temporelle
lordes ...

f. 30ᵛ

... and hee shal doo of the kynges regalies whiche shulle
take to the seid abbot of westmynstir also he shalbe nye
alwey the kyng till þe seruice of coronacioun be fully endid
and fulfillid finis deo gracias

"The maner and the fourme of the coronacioun of kynges and
queenes of england," f. 21, [*Manner and Form of the
Coronation*]; s. xv.

Edition and Other MSS: *IPMEP*, 197; to which add London, Col
Arms Vincent 25, f. 29ᵛ; on related MSS see Doyle, "Work,"
pp. 313-14; and G. A. Lester, *Sir John Paston's "Grete
Boke": A Descriptive Catalogue, with an Introduction, of
British Library MS Lansdowne 285*, (Cambridge: Brewer,
1984), pp. 71-73.

[3]
f. 33
"Privilegia westmonasterij," [*Privilege of Westmynstre*]; s.
xv ex; unedited.

[4]
f. 40
The vij principal vertues faith hope and charite the iiij
carnal vertues rightwisnes temperaunce strength and prudence
the vij dedly synnes pride envie wrath covetise slewthe
gloteny and lecherye the vij vertues contrarie to þe vij
dedly synnes mekenesse loue of thy neghbore patience charite
diligence abstinence and chastite ...

f. 44

... as it is said in the gospelle a man levith not oonly of brede but of euery worde þat goth oute of þe mouþe of gode

"Tabula compendiosa de fide cristiana," f. 39ᵛ, [A Good and a Profitable Table of the Feyth of Christian People]; table of contents, f. 39ᵛ; s. xv ex.; unedited; Wells Rev, 7: 2501 [25].
See also: BL Add 60577, f. 120.

[5]
f. 44
Forasmuche as myghty men shuld not oppresse othir by hir myght and power ne suffre themsilf neithir to be oppressid ne ouerledde of her subiettes therfor lete hem destroye and voide all evill custumes and vsagis in hir townes and lete hem make and ordeyne gode statutes ...
f. 47
... ffor the syn is not forgeven vnto tyme þat satisfaccioun of thyng withdrawen be doone and made and also men shuld oft thenk of the joyes of paradyse and on þe tormentes of helle

"a good and a profitable tretys of gode levyng to all maner astates of þe people made and ordeynede for grete men and myghty and her justices," f. 44, [A Good Tretys to Gode Levyng to All Maner Astates of the People]; s. xv ex; unedited and apparently unique; Wells Rev, 7: 2533 [135].

[6]
f. 47
First þe devill temptith hym to be proude and biddeth hym bere hym high and to be envious wrarthfull [sic] sory and to folowe vaunte to be drunklewe and to be lecherouse and þe gode angel answerth ayen god he saiþe withstondeth proude men and yevith grace to meke men for high men of porte and

of contenaunce shul be made lowe ...

f. 49

... love þou not vaynglorie and þe workes of þe synful man wo to þe þat by raveyn getist anythyng ther is no mansleer þat shal haue lyf within hymself ffinis

"þe temptaciouns of þe devill with which he temptith a man of þe vij dedly synnes and of her braunches and þe answers and defences agen of þe gode angel þat is assigned to euery man to kepe hym," f. 47, [Temptations of the Devil]; s. xv ex; unedited and apparently unique; Jolliffe, K. 6; Wells Rev, 7: 2528 [113].

[7]

f. 49ᵛ

Hit is red in þe stories and cronycles of rome þat our lorde ihesu crist was called of the people a prophete of trouthe he was of a seemly stature and gladsome havyng worshipfull chere and gladsome insomuche þat al men þat behelde hym lovide hym and dred him his heer was of the coloure of walnotys ...

f. 49ᵛ

... as þe prophecye saith of hym worthely he was feir and semely in shappe passyng all the childerne of womene

[Letter of Lentulus]; s. xv ex; unedited; cf. *Publius Lentulus, his newes to the Senate of Rome, concerning Jesus Christ* (c. 1625)]; and *STC* 15470a. 5.; and see Doyle, "Work," p. 314.

[8]

f. 55ᵛ

Words in margin of Latin poem ["Devote meditaciones de beneficiis dei"]: "Right welle beloved in god i haue me comended." From the Benedictine Abbey of Westminster, Middlesex (Ker, *Medieval Libraries*, p. 196).

Add 10336

Described: Augustus Hughes-Hughes, *Catalogue of Manuscript Music in the British Museum*, 3 vols., (London: British Museum, 1906-9), III: 312.

[1]

f. [ii]

Take ane egge and make a gret hoole yne the crowne and put forth off hit both þe whyte and yolke and forwith put in to þe shell ij sponeful of cleane ronnynge water and þen take þe iij or iiij leavis of selfigrene other wyse callyd honselyke couvir it with a little water and strayn it in to þe egge shel and put þerin so much hony as a grete peas and so moch white coperas as a whit peas and þen do ye set þe egge shel in a chafyn dyshe with a soft fyer and let it stond til it boill and þat þer ryse herof a black skyne wich do ye take cleane awey and þen do ye put forth þe water in to a fyne lynyn cloth ouer a salver or thyng what ye will and let hit go thorow the cloth with oute straynynge and when ye go to your bede lye ye vp ryght and lett on take a fether or a lynyn ragge and dropp yne to your iies ii or iij dropps yn other iie and þer to use [*illegible*] as ye fynd cause

"A medeceyn for sore iies," f. 3, [Medical recipe (complete)]; s. xv.

[2]

f. 114ᵛ

(a)

For hym that can not [*MS cropped*] take paritore off the wall parsle rottes fenell rotes and netyll croppys off ech of them a hanful ...

(b)

For hete yn the body tak borel synckfoyle borage vyolet levys stampe all to gether and strayn ...

(c)

To make good yncke take iiij vnces of gallis and breke them
yn grose powder ...

f. 109ᵛ

Item mak this stomachor ... and sow yn a bagge stychyd
materes wisse and moste the on syde with vyneger and lay
hote to your stomake

[A collection of about twenty recipes, mostly medical, some
in Latin]; leaves bound sideways, so that sequence begins at
end of volume; one or more recipes attributed to "Doctor
Wyloby," f. 114ᵛ; s. xv.

Add 10340

Described: Eleanor Prescott Hammond, *Chaucer: A
Bibliographical Manual*, (New York: Macmillan, 1933), p. 326;
M-R, I: 48-51.

[1]

f. 3ᵛᵐ

Allas i wepyng am constreined to bygynne vers of of [*sic*]
sorouful matere þat whilom in florysching studie made
delitable ditees ffor loo rendyng muses of poetes enditen to
me þinges to be writen and drery vers of wrecchednes weten
my face wiþ verray teers at þe leest no drede ne myȝt
ouercome þo muses ...

f. 40ᵛᵐ

... syn þat ȝe worchen and doon þat is to seyn ȝoure dedes
and ȝoure workes by fore þe eyen of þe juge þat seeþ and
demeþ alle þinges et cetera

"liber de consolacione philosophie," f. 3ᵛᵐ, [Geoffrey
Chaucer, *Boece*]; s. xv in; [miscellaneous marginal and
endpaper notes, ff. 1ᵛ-43, described in detail by M-R, I:
49-51].

Add 10440

<u>Editions and Other MSS</u>: *IPMEP*, 43; edited from this MS by Richard Morris, *Chaucer's Translation of Boethius's "De Consolatione Philosophiae,"* EETS, es 5 (1868); on the textual affiliations of this MS see *The Riverside Chaucer*, general ed. Larry D. Benson, (Boston: Houghton Mifflin, 1987), pp. 1151-52.

Add 10440

[1]

f. 1ᵛ

Alþouȝ it be bihiȝt to determine of anathomie þe entente was not forto noumbre alle membres particulerly þouȝ þat olde cirurgiens ben woned to diuide and noumbre membres particulerly in particuler membres and þouȝ it be necessarie to knowleche symple membres not to be ramyfied ...

f. 17

... and þe cauteries of þese places owen to be do in þe same manere after þe goynge forþ in þese membris

"þe fourþe book of anathomye and of þe fourmes of membres and of þe schapp of hem which ben to be considred with þe cauteryzynges and in knyttynge togidre of hem and contenynge in hym 5 chapitles," f. 1, [William of Saliceto, On Anatomy (the fourth book of his *Cyrurgia*)]; table of contents begins: "[T]he first chapitle of anathomye and þe schapp of þe heued," f. 1; s. xv; [miscellaneous marginal annotations, ff. 1-17]; chs. 1, 3 and 4 incomplete; unedited.

[2]

f. 17ᵛ

(a)

A generall multificats plaister for the freris fote after magister bray item comers malwis and white leued brede and

Add 10440

boile hem in rennynge water and prasse out þe water and
grynde hem smal and sethe it ageyn in mylle and þe forsaid
brad small and mynystret hote to ...
(b)
And ouer þe brache after þe said magister item hony yolkis
of eggis and sangdris ...

[Two fragmentary medical recipes]; s. xv.

[3]
f. 18
Worschipful frend bernard i þinke to make a book in whiche i
wole ȝeue by þe help of god a ful loore þat falleþ to þe
instrument of cyrurgie ne i þinke not in þis litel werk to
ȝeue þee but lyȝte fewe and assayede medycynes whiche þouȝ
þey be lyȝte and assayed ...
f. 49
... and so by good skyle and long experiment þu may be a
good leche and ellys not but ȝif almyȝty godd wolde do þat
puttynge into þee his special grace whiche godd ȝyue to þee
his grace and to me synnere forȝeuenesse of my synnes and
lyif withouten ende þat be blessyd into worldes of worldes
amen

"þe litel in cirurgie of maister lamfrank of milane," f. 18,
[Lanfranc of Milan, Little Treatise on Surgery (*Chirurgia Parva*)]; s. xv; [miscellaneous marginal annotations, ff. 18-49].

Edition and Other MSS: Annika Asplund, ed., *A Middle English Version of Lanfranc's Chirurgia Parva: The Surgical Part*, Stockholm Theses in English, 2, (Stockholm: Stockholm Univ, 1970), from Well Hist Med Libr 397, *olim* Phillips 1381 and 4783, f. 16 (Asplund does not however edit the antidotary, which forms part of Lanfranc's treatise); BL Harley 2381, f. 40; Royal 17. C. xv, f.117ᵛ; Camb, TCol R. 14. 41, f. 143; [*STC* 15192].

[4]

f. 49ᵛ

(a)

Item borage fumoter celodoine leves of emila campana scabiose veni mecum auleum quarton j ye cloke the rote and the leues and bray hem in a mortijs and late it lye 9 daies with freshe grece scabbe scall ...

(b)

The comen diaforetic þe wiche is wretyn in the antidoterie of nicoline and it is this item iiij ounces of olde oile and viij vnces of letarge of siluer þe rote of comon malwis altie fenugreke and lynsoed auleum ounces ij and make muslage of hem and put librum j of muslage in the plaister and make it as þu dedist þe toþer diaforetic it is good to dessolue hote empostemez if þe mai be resolibill it matureth and defieith it and drawit out and clensith it and dothe all the cure fro þe begynyngs is þe endinge

(c)

Ffor brekyngys in a manys hoed stampe ... and make a plaister and lay þerto and drink betoyne and it wull put out þe bonys and hele þe wounde

(d)

Ffor akynge of a grene wounde item absinth and lek and lynseed auleum and stampe hem togedir and frye hem in freshe grece and lay a plaister on þe wounde and sanabitur

[Four medical recipes (complete)]; ends: "John Soton," f. 49ᵛ; s. xv.

[5]

f. 50

In þe bygynnyng thou schal take heede to 4 that longeth to þe dome of of vryne to þe substance to þe culours to regiouns and to þe contentis ffurst loke to þe substance wheþer hit is thikke oþer þynne oþer bytwene boþe ayf þe vryne be þynne þan schal þu see thourgh þe vryne ...

Add 10596

f. 55ᵛ

... hit tokeneþ peyne in þe breste of rewme and a wicked stomake and a bad lyuer and badde lunges et cetera hic intrat explicit

[The Judgement of Urine]; s. xv; unedited.
Other MSS: BL Add 30338, f. 151ᵛ; Sloane 374, f. 5ᵛ; Sloane 382, f. 19; Well Hist Med Libr 409, f. 55; Oxon, BodL Ashmole 1447 (5), p. 186; Digby 29, f. 127ᵛ; Selden supra 73 (4), f. 107; San Marino, HM 64, f. 38ᵛ (Hanna, pp. 3-4, who gives four other possible copies); see also *STC* 22153a-22161.5.

[6]

f. 55ᵛ

(a)
Ffor to make gyngebred take halue of fair hony and putte it til a brasen panne and boile it wel ouer þe feir ...

(b)
Ffor to make char de coynce take a quart of clarified hony and ounces ij of pouder of peper and medle hem wel to gyder ...

(c)
Ffor to make playstre of plum take oyle a quart and sette it ouer þe feyr ...

f. 57ᵛ

... Ffor styngkyng breeþ seþe a litel aysel whanne þu goost to bede and waische þi mouþ þer wiþ

[A collection of about fifteen recipes, mostly medical]; s. xv; [miscellaneous marginal annotations, ff. 56-57ᵛ].
Also in: BL 33996, f. 113ᵛ (recipe (b) only), Heinrich, p. 171.

Add 10596

Add 10596

Described: F-M, I: xliv; A. I. Doyle, "Books Connected with the Vere Family and Barking Abbey," *Essex Archaeological Society's Transactions*, ns 25 (1955-60), 233 and 241-42.

[1]
f. 1
For as moche as the passage of dethe oute of the wrecchednesse of this worlde for vnkunnyng of deying not only to vnlerned men but also to religious and deuout persones semeth wonderly harde and perilous and also ryght ferfull and horryble therfor in this present matere and tretys that is of the crafte of deying ...
f. 24ᵛ
 ... the prayers of alle preestis dekenes and alle þe degrees of holy cherche helpe the so þat in pees be thy place and thy duellyng in heuenly jerusalem euerlastyng by þe mediacion of oure lord ihesu crist þat is mediatoure bituene god and man amen

"a boke þat is called the crafte of deying," f. 1, [*The Book of the Craft of Dying*]; table of contents, f. 1; ends: "Explicit tractatus de arte moriendi [*over 4 lines erased*] crystis victoriouce passion be euer youre proteccion quod [*words erased*] ordinis predicatorum," f. 24ᵛ; s. xv.
Editions and Other MSS: Wells Rev, 7: 2567 [216]; *IPMEP*, 234.

[2]
f. 25
Tobie was of þe lynage and citee of neptalym which is in þe hiȝer partis of galilee aboue naason bihynde þe weie þat ledip to þe west and haþ in þe lift side þe citee of sapheth whanne he was taken in þe daies of salmanasar king of assiriens neþeles he sett in caitifte ...
f. 47ᵛ
 ... in good lyf and in holi conuersacioun so þat þei weren

acceptable boþe to god and to men and to alle enhabiting þe
erþe

"tobie," f. 25, [*Tobit* (Wycliffite later version)]; three
lines of rubric erased, f. 25; s. xv.
<u>Editions and Other MSS</u>:   *IPMEP*, 119.

[3]
f. 47ᵛ
Mi soule magnifieþ þe lord and my spirit haþ gladide in god
myn helþe ffor he haþ biholden þe mekenes of his handmaiden
ffor lo of þis alle generaciouns schulen seie þat y am
blessid ffor he þat is myȝti haþ done to me grete þingis and
his name is holi ...
f. 48
  ... he hauyng mynde of his mercy toke israel his childe as
he haþ spoken to oure fadris to abraham and to his seed into
worldis

"Magnificat anima mea dominum et cetera," f. 47ᵛ,
[Magnificat (Wycliffite later version of Luke 1: 46-55)];
rubric: "psalmus," f. 47ᵛ; s. xv.
<u>Editions and Other MSS</u>:   *IPMEP*, 119.

[4]
f. 48
Blessid be þe lord god of israel for he haþ visitid and maad
redempcioun of his peple and he haþ rerid to us an horn of
helþe in þe hous of dauid his child as he spake bi þe mouþ
of his hooly prophetis þat weren fro þe world helpe fro oure
enemyes ...
f. 48ᵛ
  ... to ȝeue liȝt to hem þat sitten in derknessis and in
schadowe of deeþ to dresse oure feet into þe weie of pees

"Benedictus dominus deus israel quia uisitauit et fecit

redemptionem plebis sue et cetera," f. 48, [Benedictus (Wycliffite later version of Luke 1: 68-79)]; rubric: "psalmus," f. 48; s. xv.
Editions and Other MSS: *IPMEP*, 119.

[5]
f. 49
Blessid lord þat madist al þing of nouȝt kepist and gouernest alle creaturis in heuene and in erþe worschip laude and praising be to þee of alle þi werkis amen ffor graciose lord þou myȝtist haue made me a clot of erþe and gobet of metal a stone or eny suche dede creature ...
f. 52
 ... we in þankingis to þee of þi greet glorie ffor þe which haue merci lord of my trespas and euere gramerci of þi grace amen

"a deuout meditacioun a man to þenke withinne him on þe godenes of oure blessid lord at mornn or at euen as he is disposid and haþ leiser," f. 49, [Devout Meditation on the Goodness of God]; s. xv; unedited; Revell, 6.
Also in: Camb, CUL Hh. iii. 13, f. 111ᵛ.

[6]
f. 52
Almyȝti lord god of eendeles lijf þat art so ful of godenes so ful of merci and so ful of loue to synful man þat turne to þe and to þi lawis þat noon herte mai it þenke ne mouþ it mai speke so wyde is þi merci and þou lord awist of no man but good wil ...
f. 54
 ... wiþ a free herte forsake alle yuelis for þi louest so fele þi merci and goodnes þat hath noon eende amen

"A preier," f. 52, [Prayer to God]; s. xv; unedited.

Add 10596

[7]

f. 54ᵛ

O good ihesu o mercifullist ihesu o pitefulest ihesu o ihesu
sone of god and of marie ful of loue of merci and of pitee
haue merci and pitee of me o moost louing ihesu biseche bi
þilke most preciose blood which þou woldist out hilde for us
synners ...

f. 55ᵛ

... in þee to ioie and þee to praise and þee to haue for my
blis among alle hem þat louen þi swete name ihesu crist amen

[Prayer to Christ]; s. xv; unedited; Revell, 263.

[8]

f. 55ᵛ

O holi seint myȝhel archaungil of god prince of heuenli
knyȝthode messanger of þe hiȝest sowuer and hiȝest prouost
of euere during paradijs which camest to þe peple of god
into her help y preie þee helpe me synner at þe hiȝeste iuge
and defende me wiþ þin help from þe awaitis of alle myn
enemyes visible and invisible ...

f. 57

... and at þe laste to haue in possessioun euerlasting lijf
grauntinge oure lord ihesu crist which wiþ fadir and holi
goost lyueþ and regneþ god bi alle worldis of worldis amen

[Prayer to St Michael the Archangel]; s. xv; unedited;
Revell, 326.

[9]

f. 57

Holi myȝhel archaungel of god and messanger in priuytees of
the hiȝe king prince of aungels and defendir of soulis
whom oure lord ihesucrist crist god and oure lord þerfore
wolde þat þu schuldist be ouer deedli men and þat wiþ
aungels power hem defende from þe awaitis of þe feend ...

f. 58

... and wiþ alle seintis þe face of oure lord he himsilf þis grauntyng which lyueþ and regneþ þoruȝ alle worldis of worldis amen

[Prayer to Michael the Archangel]; s. xv; unedited; Revell, 325.

[10]
f. 58
I preie þe noble prince holy gabriel strengist chaumpioun of fiȝters rise þu up into myn helpe aȝens malignitees of þe feend and stonde wiþ me aȝens myn aduersaries and aȝens alle men wirching wickidnesse displaie vncouere and schewe enemyes whiche ben falseli sliȝ dryue doun hem þat ben violent þat alle myne aduersaries visible and invisible ouercomen wiþ þi help be chasid awey fforþermore holi gabriel strengyþe of god y biseche þee þat whanne drede of helle schal trouble and agaste þe outgoinge of my soule from þe bodi þat sche with þin help passe forþ in sauete and in pees bi ihesu crist oure lord amen

"An orisoun to gabriel," f. 58, [Prayer to Gabriel the Archangel (complete)]; s. xv; Revell, 324.

[11]
f. 58ᵛ
O thou greet and hiȝ prince holi raphael medicyn of god best leche and worþiest curer boþe of bodies and of sulis i biseche þe which listnedist þe bodili iȝen of tobie presentli doinge þerto þi medicyn vouche þu saaf to listne and bischyne my bodily and my spiritual iȝen and deferre not to kutte awey þoruȝ þin heuenli preier al derknes of my witt and of my soule and cure þu wiþ þin heuenly medicyn þe sikenes of my soule þat into it flowe euerlasting helþe amen

"An orisoun to raphael archaungil," f. 58ᵛ, [Prayer to Raphael the Archangel (complete)]; s. xv; Revell, 327.

[12]

f. 59

O blisful and blessid aungel of god to whos keping y wrecchid infirme and synful am assigned þat þee leding þee counforting þee exciting þee keping y schulde ouer passe þe wrecchdnes of þis pilgrimage going and þat y schulde saaf ascape þe stormy wawis of þis see y biseche þee louyngist keper ...

f. 59ᵛ

... my goostli powers and strenkþis be not togider hurt but þat y ancor rise aȝen helping bi þe þerto oure lord ihesu crist which lyueþ and regneþ god þoruȝ alle worldis of worldis amen

"dyuers praiers to a mannys owne propir aungel," f. 58ᵛ, [Prayer to a Guardian Angel]; s. xv; unedited; Revell, 329.

[13]

f. 59ᵛ

Holi aungil of god mynystre of heuenli empire to whom god deputt and assigned my keping y biseche þee bi his maieste and pitee þat þu kepe my bodi and my soule and my wittis from schrewid and wickid þouȝtis and noiose desiris and from illusions and deceitis of feendis and my bodi þu kepe from al hurt al yuel and al perel ...

f. 60

... wiþ god and with þee and with alle seintis y mai ioie wiþoute eende graunting oure lord ihesu which is blessid in worldis of worldis amen

[Prayer to a Guardian Angel]; s. xv; unedited; Revell, 329.

[14]

Add 10596

f. 60
Holi aungel to whom y am commyttid and bitaken of god to be
seen and to be rewlid and to be for perueied y biseche þee
kepe me vnfailingli and vnceesabli fauore me cherische me
couere me visite me and defende from al in rennynge of þe
feend me waking and sleping ...

f. 61
... in which y for my werk and þu for my keping to gider
wiþ blessid marie þe modir of god and holi aungels and alle
seintis we mowe be glad euerlastingli wiþ outen eende amen

"An oþer praier," f. 60, [Prayer to a Guardian Angel];
s. xv; unedited; Revell, 328.

[15]
f. 61
Heil and ioie þu swettist spirit and aungel keper of my bodi
and of my soule y blesse þee and y þanke þee for alle þe
benefetis whiche þou hast ȝeuen to me and y crie merci for
al irreuerence al vnobedience al vnattendaunce al
vngentilnes al vnkindenes and all oþer wrongis ...
f. 61ᵛ
... and offre hem into þe siȝt of myn holiest lord ihesu
crist and bringe aȝen to me grace of reconsiliatioun of pees
and of helþe amen

[Prayer to a Guardian Angel]; s. xv; unedited; Revell, 328.

[16]
f. 61ᵛ
I biseche ȝu lowli hertili and deuoutly alle holi aungels
and archaungels tronis domynaciouns principatis and
potestatis cherubym and seraphim with alle holi vertues
and y calle to alle þe knyȝthode of heuenli oostis and with
al deuocioun y praie þat bi how myche ȝe biholden sutili and
cleerli þe cleernes of goddis godhede ...

Add 10596

f. 62ᵛ

... þe loveabil and dreedful and worschipful maieste of þe holi trynyte criyng holi holi holi lord god sabaoth to þee praising worschip and glorie into worldis of worldis amen

"To alle aungeles," f. 61ᵛ, [Prayer to All Angels]; s. xv; unedited; Revell, 323.

[17]

f. 62ᵛ

I biseche ȝou o holi mychael holi gabriel holi raphael wiþ alle holi aungels and archaungels wiþ troones and domynaciouns wiþ vertuis principatis and potestatis cherubym and seraphim which stoonden afore þe cleernes of god ech day seiyng holi holi holi lord god sabaoth praie ȝee for me freel and synner þat god almyȝti defende me fro delectacioun ...

f. 63

... now lord þu puttist þi seruaunt after thi word in pees which þing he vouche saaf to graunte þat is aboue alle þingis blessid and blisful god in worldis amen

"To alle aungels," f. 62ᵛ, [Prayer to All Angels]; s. xv; unedited; Revell, 323.

[18]

f. 63ᵛ

We bisechen ȝou and wiþ al þe entent of oure soule we asken ȝoure helpis alle ȝe holi apostlis and euaungelistis whom from tyme of first vertuis of myraclis doing goddis peruiaunce and prouidence haþ chose out of alle oþere in þe world contened to make a foundement of þe newe feiþ ...

f. 64ᵛ

... we mowe deserue for to be maad not as gistis and aliens or straunge comers but citeseins and homeli at oure home dwellers and for to be myrie and glad wiþ oure lord in a

29

blissid sportful ioie þoruȝ worldis wiþouten eende amen

"To alle apostelis and euaungelistis," f. 63ᵛ, [Prayer to Apostles and Evangelists]; s. xv; unedited; Revell, 331.

[19]

f. 64ᵛ

I praie and biseche ȝou alle apostlis and euangelistis and wiþ lowli supplicacioun y aske and begge þat as verili as almyȝti god ȝaue ȝou from heuene power to binde and vnbinde in erþe and ȝou to be liȝt of þe world and þat his holi goost schulde in to ȝou descende appering in firi tungis ...
f. 65ᵛ
... and þat y folewe þe stappis of oure lord ihesu crist and ȝouris and þat y mai deserue to dwelle in þe ioie euerlastingli with ȝu amen

[Prayer to Apostles and Evangelists]; s. xv; unedited; Revell, 331.

[20]

f. 65ᵛ

O ȝe alle holi patriarkis and profetis to whom for ȝoure riȝtful lyuynge and prorogatijf of merytis oure lord haþ spokun in a ful special frendschip and to whom he schewid heuenly pryuytees so ferforþ þat ȝe illumyned and liȝtned wiþ þe holi goost schulde afore knowe and denounce þingis to come ...
f. 66ᵛ
... take ȝee in possessioun þe kingdom araied to ȝou from þe bigynnyng of þe world which lyueþ and regneþ god wiþ god þe fader and oonhede of þe holi goost þoruȝ worldis of worldis amen

"A praier to holi patriarkis," f. 65ᵛ, [Prayer to Holy Patriarchs]; s. xv; unedited; Revell, 335.

Add 10596

[21]

f. 67

O ȝe holi innocentis which bitwixe ȝoure modris brestis haue up offrid to þe maidens loue vnwemmed soulis fair araied wiþ rosis of purpur blood with vessels of whiȝt snowi fleisch plese it to ȝoure innocencie and purest clennes to vnwemmy my soule and to restore into clennes of þe holi goost my membris ...

f. 67ᵛ

... þat ȝou beinge mediatouris and oure lord beinge a piteful grauntir y may deserue of oure lord þe hundrid crowne with ȝou amen

"Of innocentis," f. 67, [Prayer to the Holy Innocents]; s. xv; unedited; Revell, 334.

[22]

f. 67ᵛ

O ȝee alle þe holi martris of god whiche bi dyuerse kindis of turmentis haue bore and suffrid and folewide þe passioun of crist in stabil constance of vnouercome feiþ and ȝe haue gete wiþ los of ȝoure blood heuenli rewardis we bisechen and crien aftir ȝoure helpis with oure lowde semblauntis ...

f. 69

... and þat we deserue wiþ ȝou forto waische oure garnementis in þe blood of þe lombe þat we mowe þerfore ioie togidere wiþ aungels wiþoute eende in heuenes amen

"Of martris," f. 67ᵛ, [Prayer to Martyrs]; s. xv; unedited; Revell, 337.

[23]

f. 69

O ȝee alle holi confessouris of god whiche bi goddis dispensacioun haue deserued to be maad knoulechers of þe

31

holi trynytees name and forto be reuerend and worschipful
sones of god we bisechen wiþ lowli soule and deuocioun oure
lord ihesu cristis fadirhode and ȝoures þat ȝe myndeful of
oure mankinde ...

f. 70ᵛ

... þat is to seie oure cleer contynuel present siȝt vpon
þe gloriose maieste of god wiþ hiȝest loue þerto folewing
amen

"Of confessouris," f. 69, [Prayer to Confessors]; s. xv;
unedited; Revell, 333.

[24]

f. 70ᵛ

Merci grace and pite we sechen and asken of oure lord god
and bi ȝou weel biloued to god alle holi virginis in heuene
we comen afore þe presence of god with knouleche biseching
ȝu þat ȝe gete from hiȝest god to us synners wiþ ȝoure
praiers and helpis of merytis þat þing ...

f. 71ᵛ

... and hens in lede to þe heuenli wedding feeste þere with
ȝou to be wiþoute eende at þe ioies of aungels graunting
oure lord ihesu crist which wiþ fadir and þe holi goost
lyueþ and regneþ god bi alle worldis of worldis amen

"Of virgins," f. 70ᵛ, [Prayer to Virgins]; s. xv; unedited;
Revell, 338.

[25]

f. 72

O ȝe holiest and blessidist maidens of crist chosen and
afore chosen of god þe fadir afore þe making of þe world y
unseli litil and vnworþi man ful of vnclennes and of
wickidnes fle to þe ȝate of ȝoure holynes and pitee qwaking
and angwisching for myn vnnoumberable synnes ...

f. 73

... graunt to alle men louyng him abiding in him and ouercomyng þorouȝ him which wiþ fadir and holi goost lyueþ and regneþ god þoruȝ worldis of worldis amen

"Of maidens," f. 72, [Prayer to Maidens]; s. xv; unedited; Revell, 336.

[26]

f. 73

O ȝe alle seintis and chosen of god to whom almyȝti god haþ araied a kingdom fro þe bigynnyng in which god loued ȝou helpe ȝe me wickid synner eer deeþ rauysche me succurre ȝe me ful vnseli eer þat þe wrethe of god lese and slee me reconcile ȝe me to my maker ...

f. 74ᵛ

... bi help of ȝoure merytis y mai come to þe cuntre of euerlasting blisfulnes graunting oure lord ihesu which lyueþ wiþ fadir and holigoost in worldis wiþouten eende amen

"A praier to alle seintis," f. 73, [Prayer to All Saints]; s. xv; unedited; Revell, 332.

[27]

f. 74ᵛ

O ȝe alle seintis and chosyn of god whos names beth writun in þe book of lijf and of þe louite praie ȝe for me to oure lord þat he graunte to me merci and grace helþe and of bodi and þat he ȝeue me feiþ hope and charite and drede to offendi him þat he ȝeue me riȝt vndirstonding parfit mekenys al oþer moral vertues ...

f. 75ᵛ

... in þe dai of þe greet doom we sauyd mai come wiþoute lette wiþ crist to þe hiȝth of euerlasting glorious liȝt and reward of alle seintis amen

[Prayer to All Saints]; s. xv; unedited.

Add 10596

[28]

f. 75ᵛ

God þrefold and oon god merciful and piteful god of passing greet benignite vouche þu saaf to heere bonerli me þin wrecchid and synful seruaunt and wiþ me alle seintis besching þi merci and þi pite for me þis praier lord which y presume to hate out afore þe siȝt of þi godhede out of a syners mouþ ...

f. 77

... noumbre me in þe noumbre of alle þi holi men which fro þe bigynnyng of þe world hidirto haþ þee plesid which lyuest and regnest euerlasting god wiþoute eende amen

[Prayer to All Saints]; s. xv; unedited.

[29]

f. 77

In þo daies a man was in babiloyne and his name was ioachim and he took a wijf sussanne bi name þe douȝter of helchie a womman ful fair and dredinge þe lord for soþe her fadir and modir whanne þei weren riȝtful tauȝte her douȝtir þe lawe of moyses ...

f. 82

... þat þei schulden bi þe lawe of moyses and þei killeden hem and giltles blood was sauyd in þat day

"a pistle of holy sussanne danyell xijᵐ capitulum," f. 77, [*The Pistle of Holy Susannah* (Wycliffite later version of Daniel 13: 1-62)]; ends: "Here eendiþ þe pistle of holy sussanne iste liber constat matilde hayle de berkinge [*another hand:*] iste liber constat domina marie hastingis de berkynge," f. 82; s. xv.

<u>Editions and Other MSS</u>: *IPMEP*, 119; provenance: Abbey of Benedictine nuns at Barking, Essex (Ker, *Medieval Libraries*, p. 6).

Add 10628

*[1]

ff. 35ᵛ-36ᵛ

Miscellaneous endpaper notes and inventory.

Add 11301

[1]

f. [7]

Letter to the Archbishop of Canterbury (from the Dukes of York, Warwick and Salisbury), *ca.* 1455.

Edition: *Rotuli Parliamentorum; ut et petitiones et placita in Parliamento tempore Edwardi R.I. (Edwardi II, Edwardi III, Henrici IV, V, VI, Edwardi IV, Ricardi III, Henrici VII, 1278-1503)*, [collected and arranged by R. Blyke, P. Morant, T. Astle and J. Topham, edited by J. Strachey], 6 vols., [(London: 1767-77)], V: 280-81 (with [2] below).

[2]

f. [7]

Letter to King Henry VI (from the Dukes of York, Warwick and Salisbury), *ca.* 1455.

Edition: See note to Add 11301[1], above.

Add 11304

[1]

ff. 172ᵛ-195ᵛ

Miscellaneous marginal annotations in books 6 and 7 of the *Stimulus Consciencie* and on endpapers.

Add 11305

*[1]

ff. 1-128ᵛ

Miscellaneous marginal and endpaper annotations in the *Prick of Conscience* (*IMEV*, 3429).

Add 11307

Described: Charlotte d'Evelyn, ed., *Meditations on the Life and Passion of Christ*, EETS, os 158 (1921), p. viii.

*[1]

ff. [v] and [x]ᵛ.

Miscellaneous words on endpapers. MS contains the following (in verse) *Meditations on the Life and Passion of Christ* (*IMEV*, 1034), *The "Long Charter" of Christ - "A" Version* (*IMEV*, 1718), and *Dialogue between the Virgin and St Bernard* (*IMEV*, 1869).

Add 11565

Described: Hamer, pp. 26-27.

[1]

f. 1ᵃ

... tenaunce of the body only as he wolde take of medicine for to hele his infirmite wherfore right as in takyng of medycyne man hath no rewarde to more ne lesse or to the preciosite of boistisnes or swetenes or bittirnes but onely as it is most conuenient and profitable to hele for soor or sekenes ...

f. 33ᵛᵇ

... in the whiche byleue by resoun we shul be sadly sette that aftir the sentence of the apostel poule though there come doun an aungel ...

"speculum vite domini nazareni ihesu cristi," f. 30ᵇ;
[Nicholas Love, *Myrrour of the Blessed Lyf of Jesu Christ*,
(translation of the pseudo-Bonaventuran *Meditationes Vitae
Christi*, attributed to John of Caulibus)]; begins
imperfectly with part of ch. 24 (Powell, p. 133), and ends
imperfectly with part of the "sacrament of cristis blessid
bodi," (Powell, p. 322); s. xv med.; [miscellaneous marginal
annotations, ff. 2ᵛᵇ-33ᵛᵇ]; Revell, 16.
<u>Editions and Other MSS</u>: *IPMEP*, 553; see also *STC* 3259-64,
3266-68.

[2]
f. 34ᵃ
Seint andrewe and other of the disciples were called thre
tymes of oure lorde ffirst he called hem to the knowleche of
hem to whan seint andrewe dwellid with seint iohannes the
baptiste his maister and anothir disciple with hym he herde
howe seint iohannes seid lo here the lambe of god ...
f. 214ᵛᵇ
 ... thou marueloust gretly of this temple that is made with
manys honde and of the precious ornamentes that shal be as
poudre byfore [*CW*: the wynde thou] ...

"the life of seyntes and this boke is called in latyn
legenda sanctorum of the whiche first bygynneth the life of
seint andrewe the apostle S S S S," f. 34ᵃ, (*1438 Golden
Legend* (*Gilte Legende*)]; ends imperfectly with part of "the
glorious life of seint katheryne," f. 211ᵃ; s. xv²;
[miscellaneous marginal annotations, ff. 34ᵃ-212ᵛᵇ].
<u>Editions and Other MSS</u>: Wells Rev, 559 [6]; *IPMEP*, 682;
[*STC* 24873-80.5]; and see Auvo Kurvinen, "Caxton's *Golden
Legend* and the Manuscripts of the *Gilte Legende*," *NM*, 60
(1959), 353-75, who notes that Add 11565 "contains 121
complete and 24 legends inserted before chapter 11" (p.

356); and Manfred Görlach, *The "South English Legendary," "Gilte Legende" and "Golden Legend,"* Braunschweiger anglistische Arbeiten, Heft 3, (Braunschweig: Technische Universität Carolo-Wilhelmina zu Braunschweig, Institut für Anglistik und Amerikanistik, 1972), pp. 23-25, on the derivations of the inserted legends.

Add 11579

[1]
f. 141ᵛ
þe ferste artikle is and confermed of þe erchebiscop stefne þat was þe erchebissop of canterbery þat we shal acorsen alle þo þat wikkedliche and aienes yift benimet holi cherche þe yift þat yt owet to hauen and alle þo þat ben aienes þe fraunchises þat longen to holi cherche ...
f. 143
 ... ywich sentence ys proued and confermed of þe pope þat was þanne and of alle þe popes þat haue ben seþen ex autoritate dei patris et cetera

"Isti sunt articuli summatum execcati de quatuor conciliis videlicet oxoniensis lammanensis rodoniensis in quibus inceritur excommunicationis sententia ipso facto et debent publicari in singulis synodis et quatuor diebus duritis post quatuor principalia capitula generalia in singulis ecclesiis tam maioribus quam minoribus," f. 141ᵛ, [Sentence of Cursing]; seven articles, followed by six further curses headed "Ex consilio domini ottoboni," f. 142ᵛ; preceded by some related Latin works; s. xiv.
Editions and Other MSS: *IPMEP*, 122; O. S. Pickering, "Notes on the Sentence of Cursing in Middle English, or a Case for the Index of Middle English Prose," *LSE*, ns 12 (1981), 229-44; to both of which may be added Add 11579.

Add 11748

[1]

f. 3

In þe name of our dere lord ihesu crist stand stedfastli in
þe callyng which he hath called þe into his seruise and hald
þe payd þer in trauayling busili wyth all þy myȝtus of þi
soule bi grace of ihesu crist forto fulfille in
sothfastnesse of good lyuyng þe stat þat þu hast take þe to
in liknesse and in semyng ...

f. 138ᵛ

... ffor a soule þat is clene stired by grace to oys of þis
worching may se more in an hour of such gostli mater þan
miȝt be write in a gret book laudetur dominus jhesus
christus amen

"liber magistri walteri hilton de vita contemplatiua," f.
138ᵛ, [Walter Hilton, *The Scale of Perfection* (both books)];
begins with note: "Hunc librum et librum vocatum gracia dei
qui est in custodia willelmi carente habeant abbatissa et
conventus shaftoniensis in succursum anime johannis horder,"
f. 1; ends: "ihesu miserere ihesu miserere iste liber
constat willelmo smyth sacerdoti cuius anime propicietur
jhesus quem post obitum suum [*another hand* johannes horder
emebat] haue merci of ȝour soule and loue wel god jhesus so
mot it be amen," f. 138ᵛ; [Hanna, p. 12, notes that the
opening of *The Vision of St John on the Sorrows of the
Virgin* occurs on f. 138ᵛ, but it is a Latin version]; s.
xv².

Edition and Other MSS: *IPMEP*, 255; owned by William Caraunt
(*ca.* 1396-1476), an important Somerset gentleman and
landowner and steward of Shaftesbury abbey, Dorset, who
intended that the *Scale* volume in his keeping should go to
the Benedictine nuns there (Ker, *Medieval Libraries*, p.
177).

Add 11748

[2]

f. 140

Oleum effusum nomen tuum þat is on englysche oyle outȝet is þi name þe name of ihesu comeþ into þe world and alsone it smelleþ as oyle outȝet oyle it is taken for ay lastyng saluacioun es hopet sothely ihesu is als mykel to meue as sauiour or heleful ...

f. 143

... and to þis day it passeþ not fro me and þerfore blessed be þe name of ihesu in þe world of worldes amen

[Translation of Richard Rolle, *Oleum Effusum* (*Encomium Nominis Jesu*)]; s. xv.

<u>Editions and Other MSS</u>: *IPMEP*, 506; and see Allen, *Writings Ascr*, pp. 66-68 and 73-77.

[3]

f. 143

Aboute þe virgyne of qwome oure lord ihesu crist toke flesch and blode we may vmthink vs of hir lyfe of þe qwech þu salt whete þat qwen sho was þre ȝere old hir fadir and hir modir offyrd hir in þe tempil and þer sho dwelled in þilk degre vnto sho was fourteen ȝere old and sho dyd þer we may witt by reuelacions ...

f. 144

... and in þe fourtend ȝere þis blessid virgyne was weddid to joseph be revelacioun of god and went aȝeȝn to nazareth and in what maner it was done þu may fynde in þe legend of hir blessede natiute

"þis is a chapitre of a boke þat þe deuoute frere menour bonauentouor made of þe lyfe of criste," f. 144, [Nicholas Love, The Rule of the Life of Our Lady, (ch. 2 of the *Myrrour of the Blessed Lyf of Jesu Christ*, a translation of the pseudo-Bonaventuran *Meditationes Vitae Christi*, attributed to John of Caulibus)]; s. xv; Revell, 13, with incorrect foliation.

Editions and Other MSS: *IPMEP*, 22.

Add 11858

Described: F-M, I: xliv-xlv.

[1]

f. 4ᵇ

The book of generacioun of jesu crist þe sone of daviþ þe
sone of abraham abraham gendride or bigat isaac isaac
forsoþe bigat jacob jacob forsoþe bigat judas and hise
breþren judas forsoþe bigat phares and ȝaram of thamar
phares forsoþe bigat esrom esrom forsoþe bigat aram aram
forsoþe bigat amynadab ...

f. 118ᵇ

... and from þese þinges þat ben writen in þis book he seiþ
þat bereþ witnessyng of þese þingis ȝostlie amen i come
soone amen come þou lord ihesu the grace of oure lord iesu
crist be wiþ ȝou alle amen

[New Testament (Wycliffite earlier version to Luke 19: 13,
then later version, with all prologues in later version)];
prologue to Matthew begins: "Mathew þat was of judee as he
is sett first in ordre of þe gospellers," f. 4ᵃ; ends: "Here
endeþ þe apocalips of joon," f. 118ᵛ; s. xv; [miscellaneous
marginal annotations, ff. 4-118].

Editions and Other MSS: Wells Rev, 2: 547 [52]; *IPMEP*, 119;
and see F-M, I: xlv, who also note, p. xli, that BL
Harley 2249 (Old Testament from Joshua to Psalms in the
Wycliffite revised version) is in the same hand as Add 11858
and "may have originally formed part of the same volume;"
and Lindberg, pp. 333-38, for MSS of the Wycliffite Bible
partly in the earlier version and partly in the later
version.

Add 12030

[1]
f. 1
Here begynnyth a book in englyssh tunge that ys called brute
of england which declareth speketh and tretethe of the furst
bygynning of the lande of englande howe it was furst
wildrenesse and noo thing there in but wormes and wylde
bestes and a countre desolate and afterwarde howe it was
enhabite and by whome and in what maner ...
f. 167ᵛ
... and the towne and the subbarbes unto the bare walles
and of alle thing that myght be bare and caryede oute was
robbede and dispoylede afterwarde the kyng passing furthe by
the cuntre aboute the brede of xx myles he wastede alle ...

"the kalendare of brute in englyssh as here after ye shall
here," [*Brut*] (regular incipit entered in index); imperfect,
ending close to the beginning of ch. 228; s. xv. Cf. HM
131[1] (Hanna, p. 13).
Edition and Other MSS: *IPMEP*, 374.

Add 12056

[1]
f. 3
Here may men se the vertues of herbis whiche beth hoot and
which beth colde and for hou manye þynges þey beth gode
quyntfoylle þat is v lef galien seiþ it is colde and drie
in tweye degrees this erbe is good for ache of mennys lendys
and for ache of hed and mouth and tongue and þrote
þat arn sore ...
f. 30
   ... and take the mylk of a ȝonge goot þat hath a kyde
sowkynge and drynke þat mylk and þe poudre togedre þe

42

mountanance of a sponfull whanne þou gost to thy bedd

[The Virtues of Herbs (a herbal probably deriving from Macer)]; s. xv.
Other MSS: Robbins, fns. 22 and 24, discusses a number of texts related to this item, including BL Add 17866, f. 5; Sloane 393, f. 87; Sloane 2269, f. 75ᵛ; Sloane 3466, f. 78; Oxon, BodL Ashmole 1438, Part II, item vii; Laud Misc 553, f. 20ᵛ; Rawl C. 211, f. 2; Camb, CUL Dd. 10. 44, f. 123ᵛ; and many others.

[2]
f. 31
þe ffirste tretys of surgerie halt withinne hy[m] generall rulys and canons and hath þre techynges þe ffirst techynge of the furste tretys haþ þre chapyttles capitulum i of the furste techynge of the firste tretys of dyffiniciones and of partyes þat beþ suggettys to surgerye capitulum ii is of qualite fforme and maners of a surgien ...
f. 86ᵛ
 ... and þe neþere ende of þese bonys beþ y joyned wiþ þe bonys of þe hande which beþ y clepyde rasceta þat beth viii bonys ...

[Lanfranc of Milan, *Science of Cirurgie*]; ending imperfectly at II. iv; section on paper, bound in the middle of vellum pages containing item [1] preceding the paper section and items [3] and [4] following it; s. xv.
Edition and Other MSS: *IPMEP*, 483.

[3]
f. 87
(a)
Item take a pynte of wyte wyne wodbynd rosemary sage feeverene a hanfull and boylle them together put therto as muche alum as a walnut and halfe a nouch of wyt cuparas and

when yt ys bolled a good space put thereto a sponfull of
hony and beytte it tyll the erbys be yawloe then stren yt
and put yt in a clen vessell so was the wonde with yt mylke
warme

(b)

Item take a halporthe of waxe put eleborum and mustele and
melt them together put thereto a penworthe of ole of
Jessys[?] and a penworthe of ole dyspyke when yt ys melted
so cleravyd clene and put yt into a boxe so mak a plaster of
yt after you have washed with the water and ley yt to the
sore

[Two untitled medical recipes (complete)]; later hand than
the rest of the MS; s. xv/xvi.

[4]

f. 87ᵛ

(a)

Item take the roote of pellyter of spayne washe it and
stampe it and make thre ballis of it wythe thy hande eache
of them the gretnesse of a plombe and ley the fyrste of them
betwene the cheke and the tothe that akythe the space of a
myle wey and ever as the water gatherythe spytte it out and
put in a fresh tylle all be donne then ley the downe to
slepe a whyle and cover the warme and sanabitur

(b)

Item take oyele benel and anoynt the therowt agaynst the
fier then take annes sede and ley it in stepe of fine
stronge venygere and let it lye so anyght and a day then
take out the annes and drye it in the wynd uppon a fayer
clothe and cast awey the venygere then eate this annyse
seede for it is good probatum est

"A medecine for the tothache" and "A medicine for the
vaynes," [Two recipes (complete)]; added s. xv.

Add 12193

[1]

f. 2

Short note to royal wardrober signed by Henry VI.

Add 12195

Described: Thomson, *Descriptive Catalogue*, pp. 193-211.

[1]

f. 66

[H]ow many partys of reson ben þer viii qwyche viii nown
pronown verbe adbverbe partycipyll coniuncion preposicion
interiection how many arn declynyd and how many arn
undeclyned iiii arn declynde and iiii arn undeclynyd qwych
iiii arn declynyd nown pronown verbe and partycipyll qwych
iiii arn undeclynyd adverbe coniuncion preposycyon and
interiecion ...

f. 66

... how many maner of nownys ben þer ii qwych ii a nown
substantyf and a nown adiectyf how ken ȝe a nown substantyf
for it may stonde ...

Accedence, [fragment of a translation of Donatus]; ends
imperfectly; s. xv ex.

Editions and Other MSS: Printed from this MS in Thomson, p.
44; cf. *IPMEP*, 308I; and Braswell, p. 36.

[2]

f. 82ᵛ

Yf þu wyl know ho haw stole þi gods wryth þis letterys in
virgyn wax and put under þin hed and he schal aperyn in þi
slepe þat hat þi gods de. so. on + s.b. [?]s. fallacon

[Complete charm, telling how to identify an unknown thief];

written in margin among miscellaneous notes and riddles in Latin and English; same formula as [3] below, but not same hand; s. xv.

[3]
f. 98ᵛ
Iff þ[u] willt knowe howe haue stollen þi gods wrythys thys leters in vyrgyn wax and put yt vnder þin hedy and he schall apere in þi slepe þat have þi gods de. so. an and s. b. s. fallacon

[A second copy]; written on lower half of defective page; s. xvi.

[4]
f. 122
I john paulen whan i was in the sete of alisawndyr i lokyd on a serteyn book that was clepyd salus vite þat is to seyn helthe of lyfe that book made aleyn the philosopher and wrot þerinne þynges þat ben verray and trewe as tellyt wel þe same book and i translated þat same book owt of grewe in to latyn ...
f. 124
   ... and he wyl use þis powdyr in his metys and drynkes þe leper schal not incresyn but abyden evere in on astat
explicit experimentum de serpente

"experimentum de serpente," [translation of Johannes Paulinus, *Experimenta de corio serpentis*]; s. xv.
Other MSS: Hanna, p. 9.

[5]
f. 124
(a)
Also ho so wele taken the powdyr of a grene eddere and make a candele of this powdyr and of talwe to gedere and as sone

Add 12195

as the candele is lithen every schal wene þat þe hows were
ful of grene edderis

(b)

Also take the pouder of the same eddere and strowe it a
monges hennys dokes or gees ...

(c)

If thou wylt make grene edderys take dragonys and sokelynge
gres ...

f. 127ᵛ

... þan take what metal þu wylt and chafe on the lettris
and the color of þe schal abydyn on þe lettrs

[Twelve charms and scientific recipes, including one in
Latin]; supplementary to John Paulen's treatise, above (see
Thomson, *Descriptive Catalogue*, p. 208); s. xv.

[6]

f. 127ᵛ

Here begynys the wyse book of phylysophie and astromye
contenede and made of the wysest philosophere and astromyere
þat ever was seyn in the werld sen syn it was be gunne that
is for to sey of the grece for in þat lond and ynglyche man
ful wyse and wel undirstandyng of filosophye and of
astronomie ...

f. 135

... they þat are in bitter peynys of hell schal se evermore
the brytnesse of this element the erth all þe blyssyd joyes
of hevene and that syht schal be more peyne on to hem þan
all the peyns of helle

[*The Booke of Astronomye and of Philosophye*]; s. xv.
Editions and Other MSS: *IPMEP*, 201.

[7]

f. 135

(a)

Add 12195

For hem þat mow nowt holdin mete ne drynke for castyng take
myllefoyle and stampe yt and temper yt with wyne, or drynke
betoyne also levys of betony playstered to þe forhed voydyth
þe hed ake

(b)

Also tak wormode and grownd yvy togedyr with þe wyte of a ey
and hony plastered to the hede ...

(c)

If þi balocs bolun or þi pyntyll be chaffed take the iuse of
morell and vynegar and anoynte it therwith ...

f. 136

... þat þe water of hym or here is in and if it go downe to
þe botum he schal dye and if it hove abovyn he scal lyve
with owte fayle

[Six short medical recipes, and two charms for determining
whether one will live or die]; s. xv.

[8]

f. 136ᵛ

(a)

Take iii oblyes and wryte in on of hem + 1 elyȝe + sabeth +
in þe oþer adonay + alpha and Ω [omega] and messias + in þe
iii pastor + agnus fons + let hym ete these iii in iii dayes
with holy water fastyng and he schal be hoyl be the grace of
god

(b)

Ffor hym þat sweat blood ȝif hym to drynk ...

(c)

Ffor to maken a man laxatyf tak burrage mercury ...

f. 136ᵛ

Tak melk[?] and whete flour or otemele play it togedere
tyll he be thyke as pap and ley it þeron as hot as he may
suffyr it and it shal a whyle ...

[A charm and four short medical recipes]; "for feveres" in

Add 12195

margin by first two; s. xv.

[9]

f. 137

Now it is for to declare and dotermyn of the xii signes and of there kyndy what ilke man is ordeynyd be weye of kynde and predestinacioun and first i do termyn of þis signe aryes þat joynys in marche and it is for to knowe þat who þat þis signe schal have a rownd face and amyabyl and swete blake browys ...

f. 139

... in may schal be fayre and of mene stature his body a party thykke and clene havyng fayre here and many thyngis he schal do

[Astrological treatise, describing people born under sign of Aries]; in other MSS, a more complete version of this treatise, sometimes called "The booke of destenarye of the 12. signes," forms a continuation of item [6] above; s. xv. Other MSS: Hanna, pp. 5-6; and cf. HM 64 generally for contents parallel to Add 12195 (including *Dieta Ypocratis* and *De corio serpentis*).

[10]

f. 139ᵛ

(a)

For to make braket take v galonys ale and i pynte hony claryfyed v unces canel ii unces peper i unce coryander ...

(b)

For to make sowre ale swet tak xii galonys ale and take a quarter of a pownd of þe rote of egremome ...

(c)

Item for a postome in a mannys body take red fenkel and sentory ...

f. 145ᵛ

... borrage viollets longbesse daysee ysop malowes and

Add 12195

mercury maydenhere herts tunge lyverwort avence and all þis
schal be sufficyant for your comyndite

[Thirty-three medical recipes, and three for drinks (ff.
139, 143); three charms to determine whether one will live
or die (ff. 141ᵛ, 142); two formulas for long-lasting nights
(f. 144)]; s. xv.

[11]
f. 146
(a)
This is the charme of seynte wylleȝam þat seynt gabryel
browte owt of paradyse fro[m] oure lord ihesu criste to
charme cristen men and women of all evlys for the wormys for
alle palsys and of þe gowte of the cankyr and of the festyr
of þe gowte ranclynge in the bone and of all maner of gowts
...
f. 147
(b) For moreyn of all maner of bestys take barly in a vessel
and ...
f. 147
(c) For to take conyes fyrst take ote malte ...
f. 156ᵛ
... menge it wel togeder with wax and oyle in maner of a
oynemente and anoynt þin membrys þerwith and þu shalt never
han lykynge þerto

[The Charm of St William, with sixteen other charms, and
twenty-four medical recipes]; s. xv.
Other MSS: "The charme of seynte wylleȝam" is also found in
BL Sloane 521, f. 272, and Sloane 962, f. 72.

[12]
f. 157
Ower lord god whan he had storyd þe world of all creatores
he made man and woman ressonabel creature and bad hem wax

and multiplye and ordent þat of them schald cum the thyrd
and þat is of þe man þat is made of hote and dry nature
schold com þe seede and of þe womane þat is made of colde
nater and moyst scholde reseyve þe seede ...
f. 184ᵛ

   ... yf a woman have a gret wombe to mak it smalle tak than
thestyl maronry[?] sowth thestyll þat growyth lowe by þe
grownd dawndelyon pympurnell and mak worts þerof and us[e]
it daylye tyle þat sche be hall

"The knowynge of womans kynde in chyldyng," [Handbook of
Gynaecology: on reproductive organs and physiology of women,
with practical advice on conceiving and giving birth]; s.
xv.
Other MSS: Robbins, fn. 35, for related texts; see also
Sloane 421A, f. 2 (I owe this reference to Prof. L. Voigts);
cf. Braswell, pp. 12-13.

[13]
f. 185
Ffyrst syth ypocras þat a lech schold tak hed of þe mon whan
sche is at þe full þan waxith blod and mary and brayn and
oþer humours þe wech be cold and moyst moyst and hote thes
sekinesis þat cold and drye and hot and drye thes schewyth
also þe corsse of þe mone ...
f. 190ᵛ

   ... and hys planets be venus and leuna thes rewll is
generall for all maner of surgery and for all maner of
postemus owtwarde explicit

"Thys bok of ypocras tech for to knowe be þe planets of
seknes both of lyf and deyth and þe tymes," [Book of
Ypocras (on planetary positions in astrological signs as
determinants of what medicine to use for a person and
when)]; s. xv; unrelated to the medical collection of the
same title (cf. *IPMEP*, 629).

Macaronic Index: Works in Latin and English

[A1]
Add 10052, f. 36ᵛ.
My dere freendis y yow pray iiij thyngis bere in your hertis away o thyng ys what fylyth a man a nothir thyng ys what makyth hym cleene the thrid is what thing kepyth hym in [*margin* hym to ordeyne] clennes the iiij is what thing drawyth hys wille to godis wille as to the frist wete ȝe welle iij thinges makith a man foule ...

"Quinta tabula hec tria conseruant hominem", f. 36ᵛ, [Fifth Tabula of the *Speculum Christiani*]; s. xv.
<u>Edition and Other MSS</u>: Wells Rev, 7: 2484 [15]; *IPMEP*, 6.

[A2]
Add 10052, f. 43ᵛ
Legitur quemdam regem quondam fuisse ...

"Sexta tabula," f. 43ᵛ, [Sixth Tabula of the *Speculum Christiani*]; ME tags, ff. 43ᵛ-45; s. xv.
<u>Edition and Other MSS</u>: See note to [A1], above.

[A3]
Add 10336, f. 6
Quilibet in arte practica mensurabilis cantus erudissime discitur affectans ea scribat diligenter que sequiuntur summarie sunt compilata et authoritate probata quicunque sunt partibus prelatomnibus et maxima longa breuibus et cani breuibus et minima ut hic [*five musical notes*] maxima perfecta valet trebus longas sine de musico perfecto sine imperfecto et si ille longe sint de musico perfecto maxima perfecta valet novem tempora ...

[John Tucke, *De arte musica*]; notes in English on musical proportions by colours: "Rede to blacke ys seque altra," f. 97; "Colours requesyt to musycal proporsyons byeþ thes," f. 98; "Blacke fulle ys perfet of þe more," f. 106ᵛ; s. xv. ex;

unedited; and see Frank Ll. Harrison, *Music in Medieval Britain*, 4th edn, (Buren: Knuf, 1980), pp. 44 and 158.

Manuscripts Consulted

The following Additional MSS were scanned but were found to contain no Middle English prose.

10008, 10009, 10010, 10011, 10012, 10013, 10014, 10015,
10016, 10019, 10020, 10027, 10037, 10040, 10043, 10044,
10045, 10048, 10049, 10050, 10051, 10057, 10058, 10059,
10060, 10061, 10062, 10063, 10064, 10065, 10066, 10068,
10069, 10070, 10071, 10072, 10073, 10074, 10079, 10080,
10081, 10082, 10083, 10084, 10085, 10086, 10087, 10088,
10089, 10090, 10091, 10092, 10093, 10094, 10095, 10097,
10098, 10100, 10103, 10104, 10105, 10107, 10108, 10109,
10113, 10128, 10129, 10132, 10134, 10142, 10143, 10144,
10145, 10146, 10148, 10153, 10154, 10169, 10170, 10172,
10176, 10177, 10186, 10197, 10209, 10212, 10213, 10218,
10220, 10227, 10228, 10232, 10237, 10239, 10248, 10262,
10286, 10287, 10288, 10289, 10290, 10291, 10292, 10293,
10294, 10295, 10296, 10297, 10298, 10299, 10301, 10302,
10303, 10304, 10305, 10315, 10316, 10317, 10318, 10319,
10320, 10322, 10323, 10324, 10328, 10335, 10339, 10341,
10342, 10343, 10344, 10345, 10350, 10351, 10352, 10353,
10362, 10363, 10365, 10366, 10374, 10375, 10377, 10378,
10383, 10384, 10385, 10386, 10387, 10389, 10391, 10392,
10393, 10394, 10395, 10396, 10398, 10400, 10411, 10414,
10415, 10416, 10421, 10422, 10424, 10425, 10426, 10431,
10432, 10433, 10438, 10450, 10451, 10458, 10459, 10546,
10574, 10597, 10606, 10612, 10620, 10621, 10622, 10625,
10626, 10627, 10628, 10632, 10691, 10692, 10694, 10697,
10698, 10704, 10707, 10717, 10725, 10727, 10729, 10735,
10736, 10738, 10741, 10742, 10743, 10744, 10757, 10764,
10767, 10769, 10771, 10773, 10775, 10788, 10791, 10795,
10796, 10799, 10802, 10803, 10804, 10808, 10813, 10815,
10817, 10826, 10836, 10840, 10843, 10844, 10845, 10851,
10866, 10892, 10894, 10895, 10897, 10902, 10903, 10919,
10924, 10925, 10926, 10927, 10928, 10929, 10930, 10931,
10932, 10933, 10934, 10935, 10936, 10937, 10938, 10939,
10941, 10943, 10944, 10945, 10946, 10947, 10948, 10949,
10950, 10951, 10952, 10953, 10954, 10955, 10956, 10957,
10958, 10959, 10960, 10961, 10962, 10963, 10964, 10965,
11037, 11253, 11274, 11284, 11294, 11298, 11306, 11321,
11342B2, 11353, 11354, 11355, 11389, 11391, 11405, 11413,
11414, 11418, 11419, 11420, 11421, 11422, 11423, 11426,
11428, 11435, 11436, 11437, 11439, 11443, 11463, 11464,
11486, 11487, 11488, 11489, 11491, 11494, 11505, 11506,
11509, 11533, 11534, 11542, 11557, 11575, 11593, 11611,
11612, 11613, 11614, 11615, 11616, 11619, 11629, 11655,
11656, 11664, 11669, 11670, 11671, 11676, 11696, 11697,
11699, 11700, 11702, 11711, 11712, 11713, 11714, 11715,
11752, 11753, 11814, 11842, 11843, 11844, 11845, 11846,
11851, 11854, 11863, 11864, 11865, 11866, 11867, 11872,
11876, 11877, 11879, 11882, 11883, 11897, 11899, 11912,
11916, 11917, 11919, 11932, 11942, 11943, 11946, 11947,
11951, 11958, 11960, 11967, 11976, 11984, 11994, 12001,
12002, 12003, 12004, 12007, 12015, 12029, 12031, 12032,
12033, 12034, 12035, 12036, 12037, 12038, 12039, 12040,

Manuscripts Consulted

12041, 12042, 12043, 12044, 12047, 12048, 12049, 12051, 12052, 12057, 12058, 12059, 12060, 12119, 12120, 12121, 12122, 12123, 12124, 12125, 12126, 12127, 12128, 12129, 12130, 12131, 12132, 12188, 12189, 12190, 12191, 12192, 12193, 12194, 12209, 12210, 12211, 12212, 12213, 12214, 12215, 12216, 12217, 12218, 12220, 12222, 12230, 12231, 12232, 12270, 12429, 12448, 12453, 12462, 12463, 12486, 12504, 12514, 12520, 12521, 12522, 12523, 12524, 12530, 12532, 13878, 13899, 13916, 13917, 13927, 13936, 13945, 13952, 13953, 13954, 13961, 13966, 13968.

Index of Incipits and Rubrics

a boke þat is called the crafte of deying	10596[1]
Aboute þe virgyne of qwome oure lord ihesu crist	11748[3]
a deuout meditacioun a man to þenke withinne him	10596[5]
A generall multificats plaister for the freris	10440[2]
a good and a profitable tretys of gode levying	10106[5]
Allas i wepyng am constreined to bygynne vers of	10340[1]
Alle werkis of þe lord blesse ȝe to þe lord	10046[4]
Almyȝti lord god of eendeles lijf þat art so ful	10596[6]
Also ho so wele taken the powdyr of a grene eddere	12195[5]
Also take the pouder of the same eddere and strowe	12195[5]
Also tak wormode and grownd yvy togedyr with þe	12195[7]
Alþouȝ it be bihiȝt to determine of anathomie þe	10440[1]
A medeceyn for sore iies	10336[1]
A medecine for the tothache	12056[4]
A medicine for the vaynes	12056[4]
And ouer þe brache after þe said magister item	10440[2]
An orisoun to gabriel	10596[10]
An orisoun to raphael archaungil	10596[11]
An oþer praier	10596[14]
a pistle of holy sussanne danyell xij° capitulum	10596[29]
a pystyl of seynt jerome sent to a mayden	10053[5]
A praier to alle seintis	10596[26]
A praier to holi patriarkis	10596[20]
A preier	10596[6]
a prologe on þe salmes of þe sauter	10046[1]
A questioun of þe peynes of helle and how soules	10036[1]
a tretes necessarye for men þat ȝeven hem vnto	10053[4]
Audite celi	10046[4]
Ave maria et cetera haile be þou marie ful of	10036[3]
Ave maria et cetera heyl be þou marie ful of grace	10053[8]
Beatus vir qui non abiit in consilio impiorum	10046[3]
Beatus vir qui non abiit in consilio impiorum	10047[1]
Benedicite	10046[4]
Benedictus	10046[4]
Benedictus dominus deus israel quia uisitauit et	10596[4]
Blacke fulle ys perfet of þe more	[A3]
Blessid be þe lord god of irael	10046[4]
Blessid be þe lord god of israel for he haþ	10596[4]
Blessid lord þat madist al þing of nouȝt kepist	10596[5]
But it is to wite þat holy scripture haþ iiij	10046[2]
Cantemus domino	10046[4]
Colours requesyt to musycal proporsyons byeþ thes	[A3]
Confitebor tibi domine quoniam iratus es michi	10046[4]
Credo in deum patrem omnipotentem i bileue in god	10053[8]
Crist in the gospel fulfilleth al þe lawe into	10053[8]
Decem precepta ueteris testamenti honora domini	10036[3]
De decem preceptis veteris testamenti	10053[8]
De duobus preceptis euangelicis	10053[8]
De semptem sacramentis ecclesie	10053[8]
De septem operibus misericordibus	10053[8]
De septem peccatis mortalibus	10053[8]

Incipits and Rubrics

De septem virtutibus principalibus	10053[8]
dyuers praiers to a mannys owne propir aungel	10596[12]
Domine audivi	10046[4]
Ego dixi	10046[4]
Euery cristen man and woman that ȝernyth to be	10053[6]
Ex consilio domini ottoboni	11579[1]
experimentum de serpente	12195[4]
Exultavit	10046[4]
Ferst take hede what veniaunce god hath taken	10053[7]
Ffor akynge of a grene wounde item absinth and lek	10440[4]
Ffor brekyngys in a manys hoed stampe ... and make	10440[4]
Ffor hym þat sweat blood ȝif hym to drynk	12195[8]
Ffor styngkyng breeþ seþe a litel aysel whanne þu	10440[6]
Ffor to make char de coynce take a quart of	10440[6]
Ffor to make gyngebred take halue of fair hony	10440[6]
Ffor to maken a man laxatyf tak burrage mercury	12195[8]
Ffor to make playstre of plum take oyle a quart	10440[6]
FFyrst syth ypocras þat a lech schold tak hed of	12195[13]
First þe devill temptith hym to be proude and	10106[6]
First the prince that is newe to be crowned the	10106[2]
For as moche as the passage of dethe oute of the	10596[1]
Forasmuche as myghty men shuld not oppresse othir	10106[5]
for feveres	12195[8]
For hem þat mow nowt holdin mete ne drynke for	12195[7]
For hete yn the body tak borel synckfoyle borage	10336[2]
For hym that can not ... take paritore off the	10336[2]
For moreyn of all maner of bestys take barly in	12195[11]
For to make braket take v galonys ale and i pynte	12195[10]
For to make sowre ale swet tak xii galonys ale	12195[10]
For to take conyes fyrst take ote malte	12195[11]
God þrefold and oon god merciful and piteful god	10596[28]
Greet abundaunce of gostly counfort and ioie in	10046[1]
Ȝe shul bileue that þe pater noster þat crist him	10053[8]
Heil and ioie þu swettist spirit and aungel keper	10596[15]
Here begynnyth a book in englyssh tunge that ys	12030[1]
Here begynys the wyse book of phylysophie and	12195[6]
Here may men se the vertues of herbis whiche beth	12056[1]
Hit is red in þe stories and cronycles of rome þat	10106[7]
Holi aungel to whom y am commyttid and bitaken of	10596[14]
Holi aungil of god mynystre of heuenli empire to	10596[13]
Holi myȝhel archaungel of god and messanger in	10596[9]
Honora dominum deum tuum the first of goddys ten	10053[8]
[H]ow many partys of reson ben þer viii qwyche	12195[1]
Hunc librum et librum vocatum gracia dei qui est	11748[1]
I biseche ȝou o holi mychael holi gabriel holi	10596[17]
I biseche ȝu lowli hertili and deuoutly alle holi	10596[16]
Iff þ[u] willt knowe howe haue stollen þi gods	12195[3]
If þi balocs bolun or þi pyntyll be chaffed take	12195[7]
If thou wylt make grene edderys take dragonys and	12195[5]

Incipits and Rubrics

I john paulen whan i was in the sete of alisawndyr	12195[4]
In primis it is for to be considred that in þe	10099[2]
In þe bygynnyng thou schal take heede to 4 that	10440[5]
In þe name of our dere lord ihesu crist stand	11748[1]
In the noble land of surey þer was a noble kyng	10099[1]
In þe pater noster ben seuen askynges þat god him	10036[3]
In þo daies a man was in babiloyne and his name	10596[29]
I praie and biseche ȝou alle apostlis and	10596[19]
I preie þe noble prince holy gabriel strengist	10596[10]
I seide in þe myddis of my daies	10046[4]
Isti sunt articuli summatum execcati de quatuor	11579[1]
Item borage fumoter celodoine leves of emila	10440[4]
Item for a postome in a mannys body take red	12195[10]
Item mak this stomachor ... and sow yn a bagge	10336[2]
Item take a halporthe of waxe put eleborum and	12056[3]
Item take a pynte of wyte wyne wodbynd rosemary	12056[3]
Item take oyele benel and anoynt the therowt	12056[4]
Item take the roote of pellyter of spayne washe it	12056[4]
Legitur quemdam regem quondam fuisse	[A2]
liber de consolacione philosophie	10340[1]
liber magistri walteri hilton de vita	11748[1]
Lorde i herde þin heringe	10046[4]
Magnificat	10046[4]
Magnificat anima mea dominum et cetera	10596[3]
Mathew þat was of judee as he is sett first in	11858[1]
Merci grace and pite we sechen and asken of oure	10596[24]
Mi soule magnifieþ þe lord and my spirit haþ	10596[3]
My dere freendis y yow pray iiij thyngis bere in	[A1]
Mynde vnderstondyng wylle reson and ymagynacioun	10053[3]
Myn herte fully ioyede in þe lord	10046[4]
My soule worschipiþ þe lord	10046[4]
Now it is for to declare and dotermyn of the xii	12195[9]
Now þouleuest þi seruaunt lord	10046[4]
Nunc dimittis	10046[4]
O blisful and blessid aungel of god to whos	10596[12]
Of confessouris	10596[23]
Of innocentis	10596[21]
Of maidens	10596[25]
Of martris	10596[22]
Of virgins	10596[24]
O good ihesu o mercifullist ihesu o pitefulest	10596[7]
O ȝe alle holi patriarkis and profetis to whom	10596[20]
O ȝe alle seintis and chosen of god to whom	10596[26]
O ȝe alle seintis and chosyn of god whos names	10596[27]
O ȝee alle holi confessouris of god whiche bi	10596[23]
O ȝee alle þe holi martris of god whiche bi	10596[22]
O ȝe holiest and blessidist maidens of crist	10596[25]
O ȝe holi innocentis which bitwixe ȝoure modris	10596[21]
O holi seint myȝhel archaungil of god prince of	10596[8]
Oleum effusum nomen tuum þat is on englysche oyle	11748[2]

Incipits and Rubrics

O thou greet and hi3 prince holi raphael medicyn	10596[11]
Ower lord god whan he had storyd þe world of all	12195[12]
Pater noster	10053[8]
Poule and my3el praied to oure lord ihesu crist of	10036[1]
Privilegia westmonasterij	10106[3]
psalmus	10596[3]
psalmus	10596[4]
Quicunque uult saluum esse ante omnia opus est	10046[4]
Quilibet in arte practica mensurabilis cantus	[A3]
Quinta tabula hec tria conseruant hominem	[A1]
Rede to blacke ys seque altra	[A3]
Sacerdos parochialis tenetur per canones docere	10053[8]
sacrament of cristis blessid bodi	11565[1]
Salutacio beate marie	10036[3]
Se 3e 3oure clepyng þis worde of þe apostil longiþ	10053[1]
Seint andrewe and other of the disciples were	11565[2]
Septem opera misericordie	10036[3]
Sequitur salutatio angelica	10053[8]
Sequitur symbalum fidei	10053[8]
Seuen dedly synnes beþ þese pride enuie wrath	10053[8]
Seuen principal vertuis longging to mannis soule	10053[8]
Seuen sacramentis of holy chirche byth these þe	10053[8]
Seuen werkys of mercy euery cristen creatur shal	10053[8]
Sexta tabula	[A2]
Speculum sancti edmundi archiopiscopi here	10053[1]
speculum vite domini nazareni ihesu cristi	11565[1]
Summe tyme in the noble lande of surrye there was	12030[1]
Synge we to þe lord	10046[4]
Tabula compendiosa de fide cristiana	10106[4]
Take ane egge and make a gret hoole yne the crowne	10336[1]
Take iii oblyes and wryte in on of hem + 1 ely3e	12195[8]
Tak melk[?] and whete flour or otemele play it	12195[8]
Teche þe vnkunnynge men goddys lawe counsyle þe	10053[2]
Te deum	10046[4]
Tese been þe vij werkes of mercy gostly	10053[2]
The booke of destenarye of the 12. signes	12195[9]
The book of generacioun of jesu crist þe sone of	11858[1]
þe canticlis	10046[4]
The charme of seynte wylle3am	12195[11]
The comen diaforetic þe wiche is wretyn in the	10440[4]
Thee god we praise	10046[4]
þe ferste artikle is and confermed of þe	11579[1]
The ferst token of loue is þat tho louer submitte	10053[4]
þe ffirste tretys of surgerie halt with inne hy[m]	12056[2]
The first besynesse and the first studie of a	10053[5]
[T]he first chapitle of anathomye and þe schapp of	10440[1]
þe fourþe book of anathomye and of þe fourmes	10440[1]
The furst of godes ten hestes is þat þou schalt	10036[3]
þe heuenes here what þinges i schal speke	10046[4]

Incipits and Rubrics

```
the kalendare of brute in englyssh as here after         12030[ 1]
The knowynge of womans kynde in chyldyng                 12195[12]
the life of seyntes and this boke is called in           11565[ 2]
þe litel in cirurgie of maister lamfrank of milane       10440[ 3]
The maner and the fourme of the coronacioun of           10106[ 2]
þe merour of holy chyrche                                10053[ 1]
þe merour of saynt edmunde                               10053[ 1]
the psaumes of dauith þat is clepid þe sauter            10047[ 1]
þe sauter                                                10046[ 3]
þese been þe v gostly wyttys                             10053[ 3]
þe sermon of saynt edmund of pounteney                   10053[ 1]
The seuene werkes of mercy ben of godes heste            10036[ 3]
þe temptaciouns of þe devill with which he               10106[ 6]
þe þre arowis þat god schal schete at domysdaie          10036[ 2]
The vij principal vertues faith hope and charite         10106[ 4]
This breue tretise is compiled for to bringe the         10099[ 2]
þis is a chapitre of a boke þat þe deuoute frere         11748[ 3]
This is the charme of seynte wyllesam þat seynt          12195[11]
Thys bok of ypocras tech for to knowe be þe              12195[13]
Title of þe crown of ffraunce is put vpon some           10099[ 3]
To alle apostelis and euaungelistis                      10596[18]
To alle aungeles                                         10596[16]
To alle aungels                                          10596[17]
tobie                                                    10596[ 2]
Tobie was of þe lynage and citee of neptalym             10596[ 2]
To make good yncke take iiij vnces of gallis and         10336[ 2]
To the kyng oure souerain lord                           10106[ 1]

We bisechen ȝou and wiþ al þe entent of oure             10596[18]
Who so wol haue in mynde þe dredeful daie of dome        10036[ 2]
Worschipful frend bernard i þinke to make a book         10440[ 3]

Yf þu wyl know ho haw stole þi gods wryth þis            12195[ 2]
```

Index of Reverse Explicits

abowte dere sowlis owre blode hert precius his   10053[6]
ake hed þe voydyth forhed þe to playstered betony   12195[7]
amen alle ȝou wiþ be crist iesu lord oure of grace   11858[1]
amen be it mot so jhesus god wel loue and soule   11748[1]
amen christus jhesus dominus laudetur book gret a   11748[1]
amen crist ihesu name swete þi louen þat hem alle   10596[7]
amen eende noon hath þat goodnes and merci þi fele   10596[6]
amen eende outen wiþ euerlastingli glad be mowe   10596[14]
amen eende wiþoute god euerlasting regnest and   10596[28]
amen eende wiþouten worldis in holigoost and   10596[26]
amen eende wiþouten worldis þoruȝ ioie sportful   10596[18]
amen folewing þerto loue hiȝest wiþ god of   10596[23]
amen god mercyful bloode precyous þi with man   10036[2]
amen grace þi of gramerci euere and trespas my of   10596[5]
amen ȝou with crowne hundrid þe lord oure of   10596[21]
amen ȝu with euerlastingli ioie þe in dwelle to   10596[19]
amen helþe euerlasting flowe it into þat soule my   10596[11]
amen helþe of and pees of reconsiliatioun of   10596[15]
amen heuenes in eende wiþoute aungels with   10596[22]
amen lord oure crist ihesu bi pees in and sauete   10596[10]
amen man and god bituene mediatoure is þat crist   10596[1]
amen seintis alle of reward and liȝt glorious   10596[27]
amen worldes of worldes into blessyd be þat ende   10440[3]
amen worldes of world þe in ihesu of name þe be   11748[2]
amen worldis in god blisful and blessid þingis   10596[17]
amen worldis of worldis alle bi god regneþ and   10596[8]
amen worldis of worldis alle bi god regneþ and   10596[24]
amen worldis of worldis alle þoruȝ god regneþ   10596[12]
amen worldis of worldis alle þoruȝ regneþ and   10596[9]
amen worldis of worldis in blessid is which ihesu   10596[13]
amen worldis of worldis into glorie and worschip   10596[16]
amen worldis of worldis þoruȝ god regneþ and   10596[25]
amen worldis of worldis þoruȝ goost holi þe of   10596[20]

bedd thy to gost þou whanne sponfull a of   12056[1]
berkinge de hayle matilde constat liber iste   10596[29]
berkynge de hastingis marie domina constat liber   10596[29]

cause fynd ye as ... use to þer and iie other yn   10336[1]
cetera et patris dei autoritate ex seþen ben haue   11579[1]
cetera et þinges alle demeþ and seeþ þat juge þe   10340[1]
comyndite your for sufficyant be schal þis all   12195[10]
contemplatiua vita de hilton walteri magistri   11748[1]
criste of lyfe þe of made bonauentouor menour   11748[3]

day lady our ayenst calais at commyng his for made   10099[3]
day þat in sauyd was blood giltles and hem   10596[29]
do schal he thyngis many and here fayre havyng   12195[9]

edderis grene of ful were hows þe þat wene schal   12195[5]
endinge þe is begynyngs þe fro cure the all dothe   10440[4]
enemyes of loue and heestis goddis of kepyng þe in   10046[1]
enemyis þyn for pray malencolyouse been þat men   10053[2]
erþe þe enhabiting alle to and men to and god to   10596[2]
est probatum good is it for seede annyse this eate   12056[4]

Reverse Explicits

euere stieþ þee haten that hem of pride the   10047[1]
explicit amen life euerlastyng þe to come may we   10099[1]
explicit hem undir men to it teche and crede þis   10046[4]
explicit intrat hic cetera et lunges badde and   10440[5]
explicit owtwarde postemus of maner all for and   12195[13]

fallacon s.b.s. and an so. de. gods þi have þat   12195[3]
fallacon s.b.[?]s. + on so. de. gods þi hat þat   12195[2]
fayle owte with lyve scal he abovyn hove it if   12195[7]
ffinis hymself within lyf haue shal þat mansleer   10106[6]
fulfillid and endid fully be coronacioun of   10106[2]

god of grace the be hoyl be schal he and fastyng   12195[8]
gode of mouþe þe of oute goth þat worde euery of   10106[4]
grace and pyte grete his for amen   10053[1]
gracias deo cyrurgie of mylane of lamfrank maister   10440[3]
gracias deo finis fulfillid and endid fully be   10106[2]

hall be sche þat tyle daylye it us[e] and þerof   12195[12]
helle of peyns the all þan hem to on peyne more   12195[6]
helle of tormentes þe on and paradyse of joyes the   10106[5]
heuene in haue schal þei blisse what men techiþ   10046[2]
hymself within lyf haue shal þat mansleer no is   10106[6]

intrat hic cetera et lunges badde and lyuer bad a   10440[5]

joon of apocalips þe endeþ here amen alle ʒou   11858[1]

lettrs þe on abydyn schal þe of color the and   12195[5]
lord þe herie spirit ech iubilatioun of cymbalis   10046[3]

membris þese in forþ goynge þe after manere same   10440[1]
moriendi arte de tractatus explicit amen man and   10596[1]

natiute blessede hir of legend þe in fynde may þu   11748[3]

payne of drede for not and hym of loue for hestis   10053[8]
pees of weie þe into feet oure dresse to deeþ of   10596[4]
pery j quod enemyis þyn for pray malencolyouse   10053[2]
place þat fro wente þei sodeynliche so and helle   10036[1]
predicatorum ordinis ... quod proteccion youre   10596[1]
prologe ende enemyes of loue and heestis goddis   10046[1]
purcharite amen tree rode the vpon deide vs for   10053[5]
purcharyte amen whomen and men cristen and vs kepe   10053[4]

sanabitur and warme the cover and whyle a slepe   12056[4]
sanabitur and wounde þe on plaister a lay and   10440[4]
serpente de experimentum explicit astat on in   12195[4]
sore the to yt ley and water the with washed have   12056[3]
stomake your to hote lay and vyneger with syde on   10336[2]
sussanne holy of pistle þe eendiþ here day þat in   10596[29]
suum obitum post quem jhesus propicietur anime   11748[1]

þerto lykynge han never shalt þu and þerwith   12195[11]

Reverse Explicits

þyself of þan more men oþer of goodenesse ymagyne	10053[3]
vs for ordeyned is þat heuen of joȝe þe to hyȝed	10053[1]
warme mylke yt with wonde the was so vessell clen	12056[3]
wiþ þer mouȝþ þi waische and bede to goost þu	10440[6]
womene of childerne the all passyng shappe in	10106[7]
worldis into seed his to and abraham to fadris	10596[3]
wounde þe hele and bonys þe out put wull it and	10440[4]
wronges open maner such justefie and occupie þat	10099[2]

Index of Acephalous Incipits

tenaunce of the body only as he wolde take of 11565[1]

Index of Atelous Explicits

alle wastede he myles xx of brede the aboute 12030[1]
aungel an doun come there though poule apostel the 11565[1]
bonys viii beth þat rasceta clepyde y beþ whiche 12056[2]
more þe and is benefice his grete þe whi for 10053[7]
sangdris and eggis of yolkis hony item magister 10440[2]
stonde may it for substantyf nown a ȝe ken how 12195[1]
thou wynde the byfore poudre as be shal that 11565[2]
to hote mynystret and small brad forsaid þe and 10440[2]
whyle a shal it and it suffyr may he as hot as 12195[8]

General Index

Abbot and Convent of Westminster   10106[1]
Accedence   12195[1]
Aldgate, London   10053[4]
All angels   10596[16] and [17]
All saints   10596[26]-[28]
Angels   10596[12]-[17]
Apostles and Evangelists   10596[18] and [19]
Archangels   10596[8]-[11]
Archbishop of Canterbury   11301[1]
Aries   12195[9]
Astrological treatise   12195[9]
Athanasian Creed   10046[4]
Audite celi   10046[4]
Augustinian Priory   10053[4]
Ave Maria   10036[3], 10053[8]

Barking, Essex   10596[29]
Benedicite   10046[4]
Benedictine abbeys   10106[8], 10596[29], 11748[1]
Benedictus   10046[4], 10596[4]
Boece   10340[1]
Bonauentour   11748[3]
Booke of Astronomye and of Philosophye   12195[6]
Book of the Craft of Dying   10596[1]
Book of Ypocras   12195[13]
Brut   10099[1], 12030[1]

Cambrigge   10053[4]
Cantemus domino   10046[4]
Canticles   10046[4], 10596[3] and [4]
Caraunt, William   11748[1]
Charles, French dauphin   10099[3]
Charm of St William   12195[11]
Charms   12195[2], [3], [5], [7], [8], [10] and [11]
Chaucer, Geoffrey   10340[1]
Chirurgia Parva   10440[3]
Christ   10596[7], 11307[1]
Chronicle Notes   10099[3]
Commandments   10036[3], 10053[8]
Confessors   10596[23]
Creed   10046[4], 10053[8]
Cyrurgia   10440[1]

De Arte Musica   [A3]
Demetriades   10053[5]
Devout Meditation on the Goodness of God   10596[5]
Dialogue between the Virgin and St Bernard   11307[1]
Dieta Ypocratis   12195[9]
Dives and Pauper   10053[7]
Domine audivi   10046[4]
Donatus   12195[1]

Edward IV   10099[1]-[3]
Ego dixi   10046[4]

General Index

Eight Chapters on Perfection 10053[4]
Elizabeth, daughter of Edward IV 10099[3]
Encomium Nominis Jesu 11748[2]
Experimenta de corio serpentis 12195[4] and [9]
Exultavit 10046[4]

Five Inner Wits 10053[3]
Formulas 12195[10]
France 10099[3]

Gabriel the Archangel 10596[10]
Genealogy of Edward IV 10099[2]
General Prologue to the Wycliffite Bible 10046[2]
Gilte Legende 11565[2]
God 10596[5] and [6]
Golden Legend 11565[2]
Good and Profitable Table of the Feyth of Christian People
    10106[4]
Good Tretys to Gode Levying 10106[5]
Guardian angel 10596[12]-[15]
Gynaecology, Handbook of 12195[12]

Henry VI 11301[2], 12193[1]
Herbal 12056[1]
Hilton, Walter 10053[4], 11748[1]
Holy Innocents 10596[21]
Holy Patriarchs 10596[20]
Holy Trinity, Aldgate 10053[4]
Horder, Johannes 11748[1]

Indulgences 10036[3]
Inventory 10628[1]

Johannes Paulinus 12195[4]
John of Caulibus 11565[1], 11748[3]
Judgement of Urine 10440[5]

Lanfranc of Milan 10440[3], 12056[2]
Lentulus, Publius 10106[7]
Letter of Lentulus 10106[7]
Letter of St Jerome to Demetriades 10053[5]
Letters 10053[5], 10106[7], 11301[1] and [2]
Little Treatise on Surgery 10440[3]
"Long Charter" of Christ 11307[1]
Love, Nicholas 11565[1], 11748[3]
Lowys de fontibus 10053[4]

Macer 12056[1]
Magnificat 10046[4], 10596[3]
Maidens 10596[25]
Manner and Form of the Coronation 10106[2]
Marginal and endpaper notes 10106[8], 10340[1], 10440[1],
    [3] and [6], 10628[1], 11304[1], 11305[1], 11307[1],
    11565[1] and [2], 11858[1], 12195[2]

General Index

Marie hastingis de berkynge 10596[29]
Martyrs 10596[22]
Matilde hayle de berkinge 10596[29]
Meditationes Vitae Christi 11565[1], 11748[3]
Meditations on the Life and Passion of Christ 11307[1]
Michael the Archangel 10596[8] and [9]
Mirror of St Edmund 10053[1]
Musical proportions by colours [A3]
Myrrour of the Blessed Lyf of Jesu Christ 11565[1], 11748[3]

New Testament 11858[1]
Nunc dimittis 10046[4]

Of Three Arrows on Dooomsday 10036[2]
Oleum Effusum 11748[2]
On Anatomy 10440[1]

Pater Noster 10036[3], 10053[8]
Paulen, John 12195[5]
Pery, J. 10053[2]
Petition to the King 10106[1]
Pistle of Holy Susannah 10596[29]
Prayers 10596[6]-[28]
Prick of Conscience 11305[1]
Privilege of Westmynstre 10106[3]
Prologue of Rolle's English Psalter 10046[1]
Prymer 10046[4]
Psalms 10046[1], 10046[3], 10047[1]
Pseudo-Bonaventura 11565[1], 11748[3]

Raphael the Archangel 10596[11]
Recipes, medical 10336[1] and [2], 10440[2], [4] and [6], 12056[3] and [4], 12195[7], [8], [10] and [11]
Recipes, scientific 12195[5]
Riddles 12195[2]
Rolle, Richard 10046[1] and [4], 11748[2]
Rule of the Life of Our Lady 11748[3]

Sacerdos Parochialis 10036[3], 10053[8]
St Edmund 10053[1]
St Gabriel 12195[11]
St Jerome 10053[5]
St Michael 10596[8]
St Paul 10036[1]
St William 12195[11]
Saints 10036[1], 10053[1] and [5], 10596[8] and [26]-[28], 11565[2], 12195[11]
Salisbury, Duke of 11301[1] and [2]
Salus vite 12195[4]
Scale of Perfection 11748[1]
Science of Cirurgie 12056[2]
Sentence of Cursing 11579[1]

General Index

Seven Deadly Sins   10036[3], 10053[6] and [8], 10106[6]
Seven Principal Virtues   10053[8]
Seven Sacraments   10053[8]
Seven Works of Bodily Mercy   10036[3], 10053[8]
Seven Works of Spiritual Mercy   10053[2]
Shaftesbury, Dorset   11748[1]
Smyth, Willelmo   11748[1]
Soton, John   10440[4]
Speculum Christiani   [A1], [A2]
Stimulus Consciencie   11304[1]

Te deum   10046[4]
Temptations of the Devil   10106[6]
Ten Commandments   10036[3], 10053[8]
Thorgortoun   10053[4]
Tobit   10596[2]
Tucke, John   [A3]
Twelve Canticles   10046[4]
Two Evangelical Commandments   10053[8]

Virgins   10596[24]
Virtues of Herbes   12056[1]
Vision of St John   11748[1]
Vision of St Paul   10036[1]

Warwick, Duke of   11301[1] and [2]
Westminster, London   10106[1] and [3]
Westminster, Middlesex   10106[8]
William of Saliceto   10440[1]
Wycliffite Bible, Benedictus   10596[4]
Wycliffite Bible, Canticles   10046[4]
Wycliffite Bible, General Prologue   10046[2]
Wycliffite Bible, Magnificat   10596[3]
Wycliffite Bible, New Testament   11858[1]
Wycliffite Bible, *Pistle of Holy Susannah*   10596[29]
Wycliffite Bible, Psalms   10046[3], 10047[1]
Wycliffite Bible, *Tobit*   10596[2]
Wyloby, Doctor   10336[2]

York, Duke of   11301[1] and [2]